Tom Ga

CU00839962

KINGFISHER
CHILDREN'S
HANDBOOK

Peter Eldin

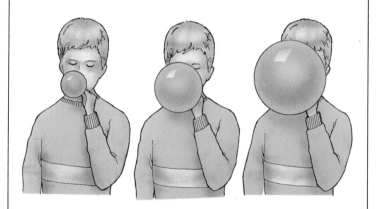

KINGFISHER BOOKS

Kingfisher Books, Grisewood & Dempsey Ltd,
Elsley House, 24–30 Great Titchfield Street,
London W1P 7AD

First published in 1990 by Kingfisher Books

Reprinted 1990

BRITISH LIBRARY CATALOGUING IN PUBLICATION DATA
Eldin, Peter, *1939*–
Children's Handbook
1. General knowledge
I. Title
082

ISBN 0-86272-433 3

Edited by John Grisewood
Designed by Graham Davis
Cover design by The Pinpoint Design Company
Picture research by Elaine Willis
Phototypeset by SPAN
Printed in Portugal

The publishers would like to thank the following artists for
contributing to the book:

Jeremy Gower (pp 6–12); Tony Gibbon of Bernard Thornton
Artists (pp15, 18, 24, 25, 26, 28, 30); Linda Thursby of Linden
Artists (pp32–42); Valerie Sangster of Linden Artists (pp43–
45); Bob Bampton of Bernard Thornton Artists (pp48–60, 63,
65–67); David Moore of Linden Artists (p.70); Jane Pickering
of Linden Artists (pp71–75). Other artists include: Mike
Saunders and Janos Marffy of Jillian Burgess Illustrations.

CONTENTS

OUR WORLD

THE SOLAR SYSTEM

Nicolaus Copernicus (1473–1543), a Polish mathematician, proved that the planets revolve around the Sun. Before then it was believed that Earth was the central body.

Copernicus described his heliocentric system of the universe, which formed the basis of modern astronomy, in his *De Revolutionibus Orbium Coelestium*. The book was written around 1530 but it was not published until 13 years later. It was to be another 500 years before his theories were generally accepted.

This diagram of the solar system is not to scale as far as distances are concerned. If the Sun was the size of a football, the Earth would be the size of a pea 130 metres away. Pluto would be as big as a grain of rice about 5 km away.

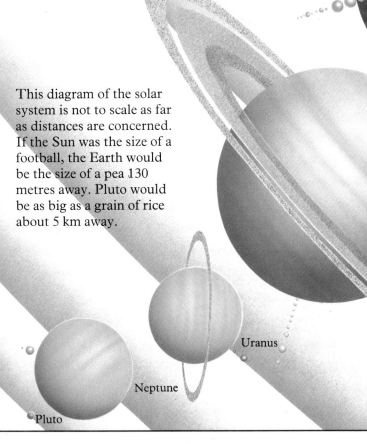

Uranus

Neptune

Pluto

Sun

Mercury

Venus

Earth

Mars

Jupiter

Saturn

Planet	from Sun (million km)	Diameter km
Mercury	57.9	4,880
Venus	108.2	12,100
Earth	149.6	12,756
Mars	227.9	6,790
Jupiter	778.8	142,600
Saturn	1,427	120,200
Uranus	2,870	49,000
Neptune	4,497	49,500
Pluto	5,900	3,000

The Solar System consists of our Sun and nine planets circling (orbiting) it. The nine planets are Mercury, Venus, Earth, Mars, Jupiter, Saturn, Uranus, Neptune and Pluto.

THE SUN is an enormous ball of gas 1,392,520 km in diameter, 109 times the size of Earth. It is estimated that the surface temperature is about 6000°C.

It is generally believed the Universe began with 'The Big Bang', a gigantic explosion some 15 to 25 thousand million years ago.

The Universe is expanding as a result of the Big Bang. Draw lots of spots on a balloon. Blow up the balloon and you will see the spots get farther apart from each other. If you imagine each of the spots as a galaxy you can begin to realize the enormity of space itself.

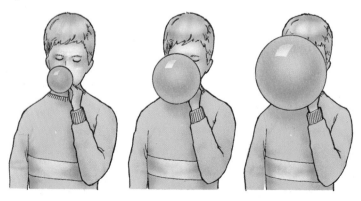

THE MILKY WAY

The Milky Way galaxy is only average sized and yet it contains a hundred billion stars, one of which is our Sun. The diameter of the Milky Way is so great that it would take 100,000 light years to cross it.

COMETS comprise small particles of dust and gases travelling through space in an irregular orbit of the Sun. A comet has a nucleus, coma and a tail, which always points away from the Sun.

METEOROIDS AND METEORITES

A METEOROID is a piece of debris, usually stone or iron, hurtling through space. If it passes into the Earth's atmosphere, it is called a METEORITE.

The Barringer Crater (below) in Arizona, USA was caused by a meteorite. The crater is 1265 metres across and 175 metres deep.

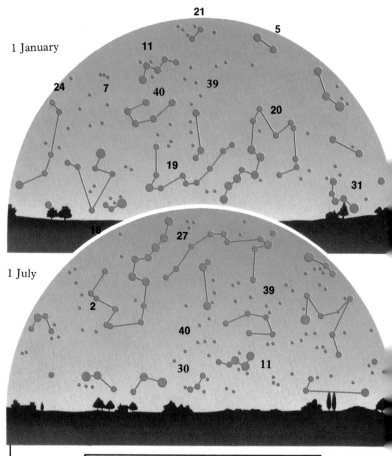

1 January

1 July

NORTHERN HEMISPHERE

These are the constellations that can be seen in the northern part of the world. The illustration shows (listed in bold type) constellations that can be seen, looking north on 1st January and 1st July.

1 Andromeda
2 Aquarius
3 Aquila
4 Aries
5 Auriga
6 Bootes
7 Cancer
8 Canis Major
9 Canis Minor
10 Capricornus
11 Cassiopeia
12 Centaurus
13 Cepheus
14 Cetus

15 Columba
16 Corona Borealis
17 Corvus
18 Cygnus
19 Draco
20 Eridanus
21 Gemini
22 Hercules
23 Hydra
24 Leo
25 Lepus
26 Libra
27 Lyra
28 Ophiuchus

29 Orion
30 Pegasus
31 Perseus
32 Pisces
33 Pisces Austrinus
34 Sagittarius
35 Scorpius
36 Serpens Caput
37 Serpens Cauda
38 Taurus
39 Ursa Major
40 Ursa Minor
41 Virgo

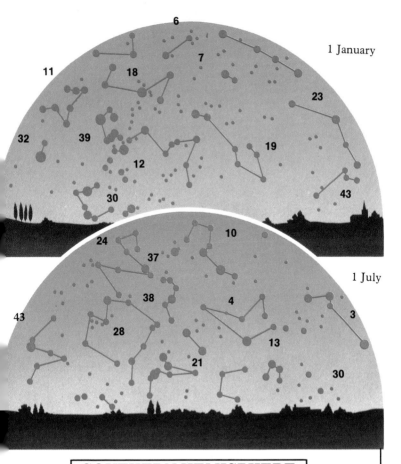

1 January

1 July

SOUTHERN HEMISPHERE

These are the constellations that can be seen in the southern skies of the world. The illustration shows (listed in bold type) constellations that can be seen, looking north on 1st January and 1st July.

1 Ara	15 Crux	**30 Pegasus**
2 Aries	16 Cygnus	31 Phoenix
3 Aquarius	17 Delphinus	**32 Pisces**
4 Aquila	**18 Eridanus**	33 Pisces Austrinus
5 Cancer	**19 Gemini**	34 Sagitta
6 Canis Major	20 Grus	35 Sagittarius
7 Canis Minor	**21 Hercules**	36 Sculptor
8 Capricornus	22 Hydra	**37 Scorpius**
9 Carina	**23 Leo**	**38 Serpens**
10 Centaurus	**24 Libra**	**39 Taurus**
11 Cetus	25 Lupus	40 Triangulum
12 Corona	26 Monoceros	41 Triangulum
Borealis	27 Octans	Australe
13 Corvus	**28 Ophiuchus**	42 Vela
14 Crater	29 Orion	**43 Virgo**

11

THE MOON

The Moon is the closest natural body to the Earth in the sky. It is 384,000 km from the Earth and has a diameter of 3476 km. The Moon is not a planet but a natural satellite of the Earth. It takes 27 days and 8 hours for the Moon to complete one orbit of Earth.

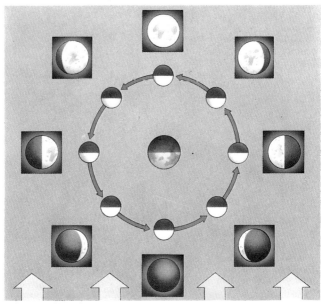

Phases of the Moon occur because different parts of it reflect sunlight as the Moon orbits the Earth. The Moon appears to change shape.

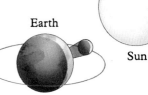

A SOLAR ECLIPSE occurs when the Moon passes between the Sun and the Earth.

A LUNAR ECLIPSE occurs when the Earth is between the Sun and the Moon, so the Earth's shadow causes the Moon to be less visible.

ASTRONOMY FACTS

QUASAR is an abbreviation for quasi-stellar-object. Quasars were first discovered in 1963 by radio astronomers. Quasars may be new galaxies in the early stages of development.

Many quasars are estimated to be some 10,000 million light years from Earth. This means we are seeing them as they were 10,000 million years ago – long before the Earth itself was born.

A galaxy is an enormous group of stars, planets, gas and dust. Our Solar System is a small part of the Milky Way galaxy, one of billions of galaxies in the Universe.

Light from the Moon takes 1.3 seconds to reach Earth. Light from the Sun takes 8.5 minutes to reach Earth Light from Alpha Centuri, the nearest star apart from the Sun, takes 4.3 years to reach Earth. Light from the M31 Galaxy in Andromeda, the most distant object visible to the naked eye, takes 2,200,000 years to reach Earth.

A BLACK HOLE could be one result of the death of a star. When the star has collapsed its gravity becomes so strong that it starts spinning. At this stage it is known as a Pulsar (pulsating star) for it emits a beam of energy at regular intervals. The matter of a pulsar is so dense that one teaspoonful of it would weigh one million tonnes. As the matter continues to pack itself even tighter its gravitational pull is increased until none of its energy, not even light, can escape its pull.
The existence of black holes was predicted by the great physicist Albert Einstein. The first black hole, Cygnus X-1, was discovered in 1972 some 7000 light years from Earth.

Because distances in space are so great, astronomers use LIGHT YEARS to measure distance. A light year is the distance that light can travel in one year. As light travels at 300,000 km in one second, a light year is about 9.5 million, million km.

Speed of light = 299,792.458 km per second
Light year   = 9,460,528,405,000 km
Parsec   = 3.26 light years

THE EARTH

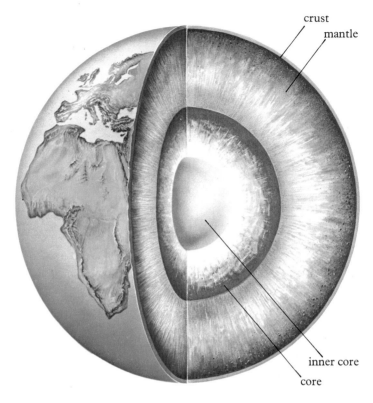

crust
mantle
inner core
core

The distance around the Earth is 40,090 km at the Equator. Around the poles the distance is 40,070 km.

The outer crust of the Earth ranges in thickness from about five kilometres in some parts of the ocean to about 80 km in mountainous regions.

Beneath the Earth's crust there is a layer of solid rock, some 2800 km thick, called the mantle.

The core is believed to be a large ball of iron, solid in the centre but molten on the outside.

The crust is made up of a number of plates which float on the mantle, like blocks of wood floating on water. These plates have been moving slowly since the beginning of time.

At one time all the continents were one vast land mass which geologists have named Pangaea, from the Greek words 'pan' (all) and 'gaia' (land). About two hundred million years ago it began to divide until eventually the continents of today drifted into their present positions.

The continents have been slowly drifting on the surface of the Earth since our planet became solid. About 200 million years ago they were joined together in Pangaea. Then the Atlantic opened up, separating the Americas from Africa and Europe.

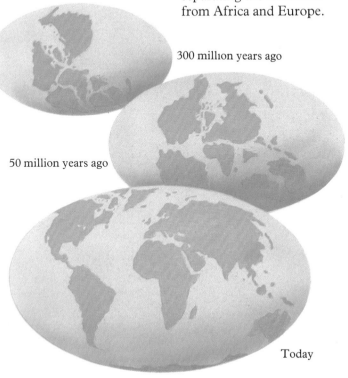

300 million years ago

50 million years ago

Today

THE CAUSE OF EARTHQUAKES

In some regions the Earth's plates have pushed against each other to form mountain ranges. In other places one plate has been forced beneath the other and this forms deep trenches. Sometimes the plates grind against each other to form faults which are the cause of many earthquakes.

● THE RICHTER SCALE, used for measuring the amount of energy released by earthquakes, was devised by Charles F. Richter. It is numbered from 1 to 10 in the order of intensity.

The intensity of earthquakes is measured by an instrument called a seismograph.

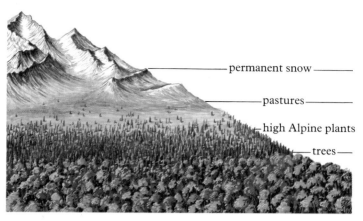

permanent snow
pastures
high Alpine plants
trees

HIGH MOUNTAINS

Name	Range	Height (m)
Everest	Himalaya-Nepal/Tibet	8848
Godwin Austen	Pakistan/India	8611
Kanchenjunga	Himalaya-Nepal/India	8597
Aconcagua	Andes-Argentina	6960
McKinley	Alaska Range	6194
Kilimanjaro	Tanzania	5895
Elbruz	Caucasus-USSR	5633
Vinson Massif	Antarctica	5140
Jaja	New Guinea	5029
Mont Blanc	Alps-France	4807

FACTS ABOUT VOLCANOES

ACTIVE VOLCANOES: There are about 535, 80 below the sea.

LARGEST KNOWN ERUPTION: Tambora, Indonesia, in 1815. The volcano threw out about 150 cubic kilometres of matter.

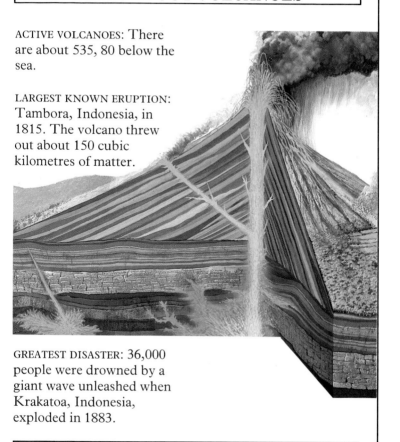

GREATEST DISASTER: 36,000 people were drowned by a giant wave unleashed when Krakatoa, Indonesia, exploded in 1883.

TYPES OF VOLCANIC ERUPTIONS

Vulcanian Strong ejections of clouds of ash and lava.
Icelandic Gentle eruptions from fissures in the Earth's crust.
Strombolian Constant small eruptions of clouds of hot lava.
Hawaiian Frequent eruptions of liquid lava from a central vent.
Plinian Violent explosions of gas and ash.
Pelean Most explosive form with huge clouds and streams of ash, steam and lava emitted from side vents.
Vesuvian Strong explosions emitting vast quantities of ash.

DESERTS

Not all deserts are hot and sandy. Some are cold, and some are rocky. But all are very dry. About a fifth of the Earth's land surface is desert. It is very difficult for plants or animals to live in such places. Many desert animals shelter from the sun by day and come out only at night. Some never drink, but get all the moisture they need from their food. Some plants, like the cactus, store moisture in their fleshy stems. The world's largest desert is the Sahara in Africa which is 9,096,000 sq. km. The Australian Desert is 1,550,000 sq. km.

Badwater in the Death Valley of California is the lowest point (86 metres below sea level) in the USA.

THE POLES

The areas of the Earth around the North and South Poles do not receive as much of the Sun's heat as other parts. As a result these regions are extremely cold and permanently covered with ice. The South Pole is about 2800 metres above sea level but almost 2700 metres of that height is ice.

The Equinox, when the Earth is upright, not tilted

THE ARCTIC is an ice-covered sea. This enabled the American nuclear submarine *Nautilus* to cross the North Pole beneath the surface in 1958.

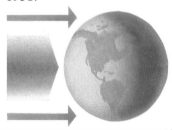

OCEANS

Pacific Ocean

Indian Ocean

Oceans cover nearly three-quarters of the Earth's surface. Oceans are always losing water, drawn up into the air by the Sun's heat. Most returns as rain. There are four oceans. The largest and deepest is the Pacific (181 million sq km). The oceans are never still. Winds crinkle their surface into waves. Currents flow, like rivers, through the oceans. Every day the ocean surface rises and falls with the tides. Oceans are home to countless living things from tiny plants called plankton to the Blue Whale, the largest animal in the world.

MAKE AN ICEBERG

Only one-eighth of an iceberg is visible above the surface of the water.

Make your own iceberg to show how much is hidden. Fill a plastic tumbler with water and place it in the freezer compartment of a fridge.

When the water has frozen, hold the tumbler under warm running water until the block of ice drops out.

Place your 'iceberg' in a bowl of water. You will see immediately that most of its bulk is below the water line.

Imagine that mass of ice over ten times the size of a normal house.

HOW THE WORLD GOT ITS SHAPE

The Earth is slightly flatter at the poles than it is at the Equator.

Take a thin strip of paper about 50 cm long. Glue the ends. Push a long pencil through the loop. Hold the pencil tightly at the top of the loop and loosely at the bottom. Push the pencil into the chuck of a drill. (First ask an adult if you can do this.)

Switch on the drill. When the loop is spinning it forms an oval shape, the top and bottom of which are quite flat.

Much the same thing has happened to the world as it spins on its axis.

THREATENED AREAS

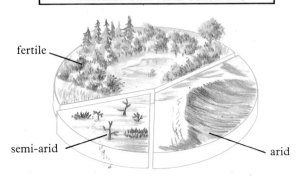

fertile

semi-arid

arid

land area of the Earth

DESERTIFICATION is not caused by changes in the climate but by human actions. Some 20,000 sq km of arid or semi-arid land becomes desert each year. The four causes of desertification are over-cultivation, over-grazing, clearance of forests and inefficient irrigation. The biggest single area under threat from the effects of desertification is in the USA, notably California, Nevada and Arizona.

The GIANT'S CAUSEWAY in north-east Ireland was formed by lava some fifty million years ago. It consists of some 40,000 basalt columns ranging in diameter from 35 to 50 cm. According to folklore the rocks were formed by Finn MacCool who laid a pathway from Ireland (to Scotland).

ANGEL FALLS is the world's highest waterfall. It is located on Mount Auyantepui, a plateau in south-eastern Venezuela. It has a total height of 979 metres. James Angel, an American aviator, discovered the falls in 1935 when he was flying through one of the canyons of the plateau looking for gold.

▼ THE GRAND CANYON, through which flows the Colorado River, is one of the world's most spectacular natural features. The canyon, in north-west Arizona, USA, began to form millions of years ago and it is getting deeper all the time. The canyon is 446 km long, 2133 metres deep and varies in width from six to twenty kilometres.

▼ LAKE TITICACA at 3812 metres above sea level, is the highest navigable lake in the world. Titicaca, half of which is in Peru and half in Bolivia, measures 193 by 72 km. The name of the lake comes from the wildcats that live on the islands in the lake and swim to the mainland for food. 'Titi' means 'wildcat' and 'karka' means 'rock'. The lakeside reeds are made into boats and huts.

▲ AURORA Brilliantly glowing coloured lights can often be seen in the polar regions. At the North Pole they are called aurora borealis – the northern dawn. Similar lights in the southern polar regions are called aurora australis. The lights are caused by electrical discharges as magnetic energy from the Sun invades the upper atmosphere

THE DEAD SEA on the Israel-Jordan border is 395 metres below sea level, the lowest place on the Earth's surface. For about a third of its 80-km length it is only a few feet deep. Nothing can live in the Dead Sea for it contains more than six times the amount of mineral salts found in ordinary sea water. This makes the water so dense that even non-swimmers float on it. The mineral salts have built up because the sea has no outlet and the Sun's heat causes continual evaporation.

EGG AFLOAT

Place an egg in a glass of water and see it sink to the bottom. Remove the egg and stir in three tablespoons of salt. Return the egg to the water and watch it float on the surface.

The salt in the water supports the egg, just as the salt in the Dead Sea will support a person.

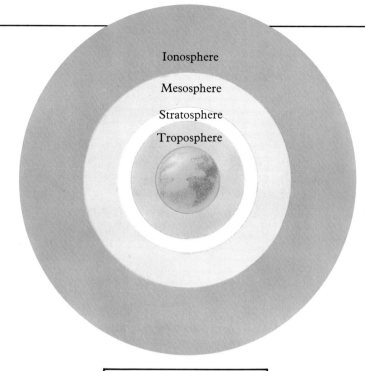

Ionosphere

Mesosphere

Stratosphere

Troposphere

CLIMATE

The atmosphere is made up of bands of gases extending for about 150 km above the Earth's surface. It protects our planet from the Sun's intense heat and harmful short-wave emissions. It also helps keep the warmth from escaping into space at night. If there were no atmosphere, day time temperatures on Earth could be over 110°C and at night they would drop to below − 145°C.

The nearness of oceans and seas affects climate. The waters are cooler than land during the summer months and warmer than land in colder weather. Some places are also affected by sea currents that bring warm or cold conditions to the region.

THE WATER CYCLE

The word's rivers discharge into the sea thirteen million cubic kilometres of water every hour. The Sun's warmth on the sea causes some of the water to evaporate. This water vapour rises and condenses into droplets of water which form clouds. The colder the air the less water vapour it can hold. Eventually it reaches 'saturation point'. If the air cools any further it cannot hold all the vapour, so it falls as rain or snow. This snow or rain drains into the rivers to complete the cycle.

NAMING CLOUDS

The three principal cloud names are:

CIRRUS — a hair-like, or streaky cloud.

CUMULUS — a pile of fluffy cloud.

STRATUS — a layer or sheet of cloud.

A prefix is often added – indicating height:

CIRRO — a high cloud (over 6000 m).

ALTO — a medium height cloud (2000 to 6000 m).

STRATO — a low cloud (up to 2000 m).

NIMBO — rain cloud.

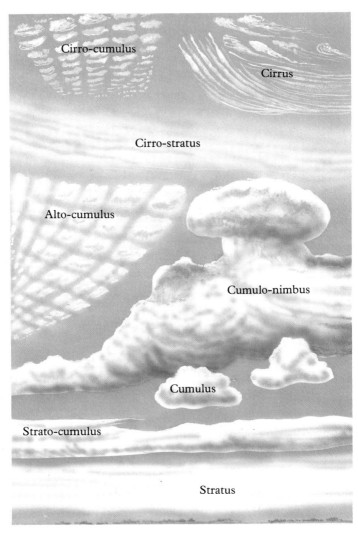

Cirro-cumulus

Cirrus

Cirro-stratus

Alto-cumulus

Cumulo-nimbus

Cumulus

Strato-cumulus

Stratus

WORLD WINDS

CHINOOK Warm, dry wind on the eastern side of Rocky Mountains, USA.
MISTRAL Blows down the Rhone valley in France towards Mediterranean.
SIROCCO Warm wind going north across Sahara and Mediterranean.
FÖHN Warm, dry wind coming off the northern slopes of Alps.
BRICKFIELDER Hot wind of south-east Australia.
BURAN Strong wind of Russia and central Asia.
PAMPERO Cold wind which blows from the Andes across Argentina.
SHAMAL Hot, dry summer wind of Iraq and the Gulf.

MAKE A CLOUD

With just a saucepan of water, some ice cubes and a metal plate you can see how rain clouds form. (Wear oven gloves and get the permission of an adult before trying this experiment.)

Place the ice cubes on the metal plate. Now boil some water in the saucepan and you will see steam forming. This steam, or water vapour, vanishes into the air. But if you hold the ice-filled metal plate over the saucepan you will see droplets forming on the underside of the plate. This is similar to the way that rain is formed, the water vapour rises until it reaches a colder atmosphere when it becomes rain.

CLOUD FACTS

- An average cloud weighs about 50,000 tonnes.
- Winds carry clouds along at speeds of between 18 and 110 km/h.
- A raindrop hits Earth at about 30 km/h.
- The largest raindrop recorded was as big as a pea.
- To find how far a thunderstorm is away from you count the number of seconds between the flash of lightning and the crash of thunder. Divide this number by three and the answer is the distance in kilometres of the storm.

THE SEASONS

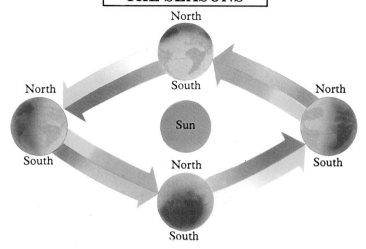

Seasons occur because of the Earth's position in relation to the Sun. As the Earth is tilted on its axis places receive varying amounts of sunlight depending upon whether the tilt is towards or away from the Sun as the Earth orbits around it. When it is summer in the southern hemisphere, it is winter in the northern half of the world. The diagram shows this by using 'warm' to 'cool' colours.

HOTTEST, COLDEST, WETTEST

The hottest place on Earth is in Libya, North Africa. In 1922 the temperature reached 58°C.

The coldest place on Earth is the Antarctic, as cold as −89°C.

Cherrapunji in India holds the record for **most rain** in a month (9299 mm) and in a year (24,461 mm).

The world's **heaviest hailstones** were reported in 1986, in Bangladesh. They weighed more than one kilogram each (almost as much as a baseball).

A warm water current called the North Atlantic Drift keeps winters in Britain milder than in mainland Europe.

LIGHTNING

Lightning is a gigantic electric spark. If the two terminals of a battery are placed together, a spark will jump from one to the other. Lightning is formed in a similar way. Electrical energy builds up in the clouds until eventually there is a discharge from one cloud to another or from a cloud to the ground.

● The heat produced by the flash of lightning expands the air so quickly it causes a bang of thunder.

● The odds against anyone being struck by lightning are about four million to one.

● Around the world there are some 6000 flashes of lightning every minute and 16 million thunderstorms a year.

● A flash of lightning generates almost 500 million volts of electricity.

SNOWFLAKES

Under a microscope snowflakes reveal a wonderworld of intricate patterns. They are all formed of six-sided or six pointed patterns but – incredible though it may seem – every one is completely different. Each snowflake is formed around a small particle of dust or some other matter.

RAINBOW

A rainbow forms because raindrops act like prisms and break up white light into the different colours of the spectrum. The colours of a rainbow always appear in the same order: red, orange, yellow, green, blue, indigo and violet.

WEATHER FORECASTS

The pressure that air exerts on the Earth's surface is measured in millibars. The pressure changes from one place to another. These differences help meteorologists to determine weather.

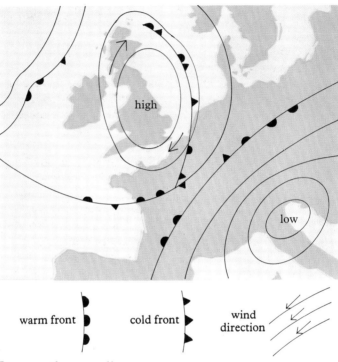

warm front   cold front   wind direction

On a weather map lines are drawn to join places of equal pressure, measured in millibars. These lines are called 'isobars'. Winds blow from areas of high pressure to areas of low pressure. When there are big differences in pressure the isobars are closer and the winds are stronger.

An area of high pressure is usually a sign of settled weather with clear skies. In low pressure areas the weather is usually wet and windy and unsettled.

In the northern hemisphere winds blow clockwise around the highs and anti-clockwise around the lows – the opposite in the southern hemisphere.

If you stand with your back to the wind the nearest area of low pressure will be to your left if you are in the northern hemisphere and to the right if you are in the southern hemisphere.

YOUR OWN WEATHER STATION

With your own weather station you can keep an accurate daily record. Take readings from your instruments at least twice a day and write down your findings in a diary. If you have a computer, record the figures on that so you can keep a more accurate check on trends and changes.

RAIN GAUGE All you need is a jar and a plastic funnel. Mark the jar in centimetres so you can keep a record.

To get an indication of the WIND SPEED you need a small sheet of thick card hanging on a wire. As the wind blows, the card will move and the angle at which it swings gives you an idea of how strong it is.

MAKE A SIMPLE BAROMETER with a jar, a balloon, an elastic band, a drinking straw and a small piece of card. Put them together as shown, making certain that the balloon is stretched taut over the top of the jar and held firmly in place with the elastic band. Glue the straw to the bent card and glue the card to the jar. A hand-written gauge on a card will allow you to observe any changes in air pressure as the straw indicator moves up or down.

High air pressure means fine weather and low pressure indicates bad weather to come.

THE LIVING WORLD

YOUR AMAZING BODY

The human body contains 11 kg of carbon, 38 litres of water, sufficient phosphorus to make 2000 match heads, 1.5 kg of calcium, enough fat to make ten bars of soap and enough iron to make a 3-cm long nail.

vertebrae

- About 70 per cent of a person's body weight is made up of water.

- It is impossible to sneeze with your eyes open.

- Blinking causes your eyes to be closed for half an hour each day.

bones of the feet

- The purpose of yawning is to send an extra supply of oxygen to the brain when you are tired.

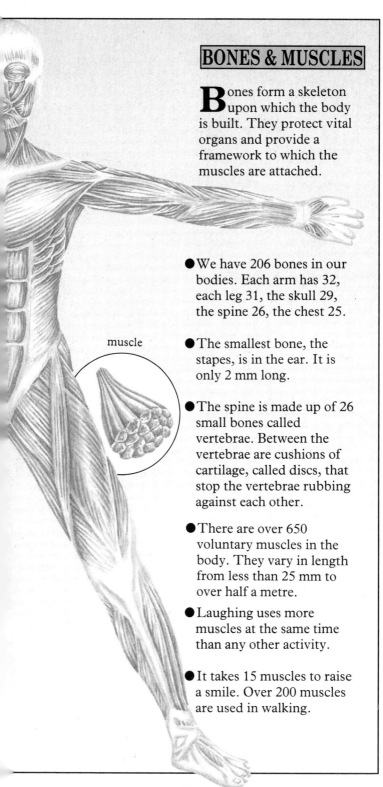

BONES & MUSCLES

Bones form a skeleton upon which the body is built. They protect vital organs and provide a framework to which the muscles are attached.

muscle

- We have 206 bones in our bodies. Each arm has 32, each leg 31, the skull 29, the spine 26, the chest 25.

- The smallest bone, the stapes, is in the ear. It is only 2 mm long.

- The spine is made up of 26 small bones called vertebrae. Between the vertebrae are cushions of cartilage, called discs, that stop the vertebrae rubbing against each other.

- There are over 650 voluntary muscles in the body. They vary in length from less than 25 mm to over half a metre.

- Laughing uses more muscles at the same time than any other activity.

- It takes 15 muscles to raise a smile. Over 200 muscles are used in walking.

KIDNEYS

The kidneys filter the waste products of the body from the blood.

● Most of the water is returned to the circulation together with important chemicals. Water that is not retained combines with waste products to form urine.

● Blood goes through the kidneys at a rate of 130 litres a day.

LUNGS

The lungs breathe in oxygen from the air to provide food for the blood. You breathe out the carbon dioxide gas that has been removed from your blood. Lungs have an area of 70 sq.m.

● In 24 hours a healthy adult breathes 23,000 times, taking in 120.3 cubic metres of air. He or she produces 2.0 litres of saliva and 1.14 litres of perspiration.

HEART AND BLOOD

The heart is a muscle which pumps blood around your body. An adult human heart weighs about 300 grams, and beats over 100,000 times a day.

● The left hand side of the heart takes blood from the lungs and pumps it around the body. The right side takes blood from the body and pumps it to the lungs.

● It takes about 45 seconds for the blood from the heart to go around the body and back to the heart again.

● Blood is actually four different substances – plasma, red cells, white cells and platelets.

● The colouring of red cells is caused by an iron containing substance called haemoglobin.

● Red cells carry oxygen from the lungs around the body.

● There are five types of white blood cells (leucocytes) but there is only one white cell to every 700 red cells.

● The liquid in which blood cells float is called plasma. Plasma is 90% water.

● There are four main blood groups A, B, AB and O. World wide, group O is the most common but other groups are more common in various countries.

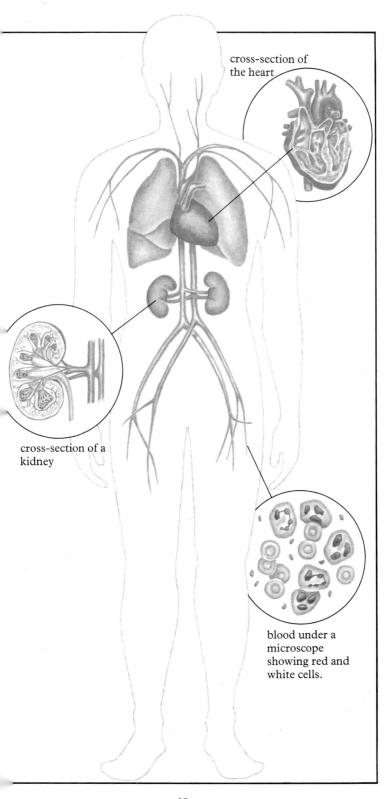

cross-section of
the heart

cross-section of a
kidney

blood under a
microscope
showing red and
white cells.

OUR SENSES

All the information you receive about the world about you comes through your senses. The five senses are sight, hearing, smell, taste and touch.

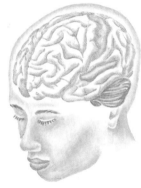

The brain is the body's control centre. The largest area of the brain is the cortex. It directs all your voluntary movements, receives messages from the sense organs and is responsible for your intelligence. Sensations such as sight, hearing, smell and taste are received by special sensory areas on the cortex (see diagrams).

EYES

● Rays of light from the object being looked at pass through the cornea and are focused by the lens on to the retina. Information from light sensitive nerve endings in the retina are transmitted by the optic nerve to the brain. Between the cornea and the lens is the iris which controls the amount of light entering the eye.

● On the surface of the retina there are 132 million light sensitive cells. Most of these are rod shaped and are used for black and white vision; the remaining seven million are cone shaped and used for colour vision.

● Carrots are rich in Vitamin A which is needed to make light-sensitive chemicals inside rods and cones.

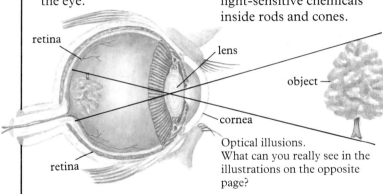

retina

lens

object —

cornea

retina

Optical illusions.
What can you really see in the illustrations on the opposite page?

THE BLIND SPOT ●

There are no light sensitive cells where the optic nerve meets the retina, so no image is formed at this point, which is known as the blind spot.

To show the existence of the blind spot close your left eye and look at the cat. Now move the page away from you keeping your eye focused on the cat. The spot on the right will disappear as its image falls on the blind spot.

HAIR AND NAILS

All hairs develop from small holes called follicles which contain the hair root.

● Hairs grow at the rate of some 12 mm a month and most hairs can grow to a length of 700 mm before they fall out.

Blondes have an average of 140,000 hairs on their head, brunettes 110,000, black haired people 108,000 and redheads 90,000. Hair colour is inherited from your parents.

● About 50 hairs fall from your head each day.

● Finger nails grow at a rate of about three millimetres a month.

● The cuticles – half moons – at the base of your nails look white because this part is not firmly attached to the skin beneath.

HEARING

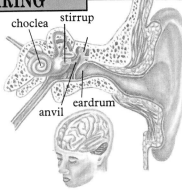

The ear channels sound vibrations down to the ear drum. These vibrations are amplified by three small bones, the hammer, anvil and stirrup. In the next part of the ear, the cochlea, there are two small membranes, which change the vibrations into nerve impulses which the auditory nerve transmits to the brain.

Inside the ear are three semi-circular canals and two organs, which control balance.

TASTE AND SMELL

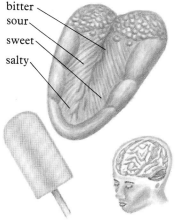

The tongue can discern only four basic tastes: salt, sweet, sour and bitter. Each taste is detected by taste buds in specific areas of the tongue. Put a little bit of salt in the centre of your tongue. You won't be able to taste it for there are no taste buds in this area.

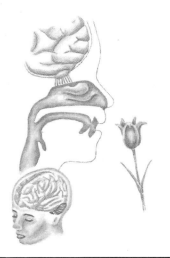

Smell receptors are in the upper half of your nose, in the nasal cavity. Each receptor has a tiny hair covered in sticky mucus. Scent particles dissolve in the mucus and the receptors send messages to the cortex.

Humans have a very poor sense of smell compared with other animals.

TEETH

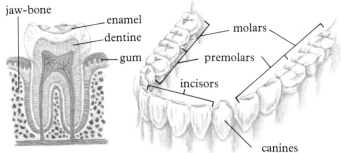

jaw-bone
enamel
dentine
gum
molars
premolars
incisors
canines

By the age of two and a half a child has 20 'milk' teeth. These begin to loosen after about six years and 32 permanent teeth take their place.

● Both teeth and gums should be brushed at least twice a day to remove bits of food and stop the build up of harmful plaque. Plaque is a sticky substance containing millions of bacteria that attack the teeth and gums.

● In front of the mouth are the incisors used for cutting and biting. To each side of the mouth are the canine teeth which are used for tearing and shredding. At the back of the mouth are the pre-molars and molars which are used for chewing and grinding food.

DIGESTION

As food is broken up by the teeth, saliva is secreted from the salivary glands. Saliva helps turn some of the starch in the food into sugar and makes the food easier to swallow. Other chemicals in the digestive juices work on the food when it reaches the stomach. It is then squeezed into the duodenum where bile from the liver and juices from the pancreas help break down the food. It then goes into the intestine where digestion is completed and items needed by the body pass into the blood stream.

SKIN

The skin of an adult human covers an area of more than 1.5 square metres and weighs about 2.25 kilos.

Skin colouring is determined by a substance called melanin. Whether you have a dark or a light skin depends upon the activity of the melanin which protects the skin from ultra-violet rays.

A piece of skin about the size of a 5p coin contains a metre of blood vessels, at least 35 nerve endings, 80 sweat glands and over three million cells.

TEST YOUR SENSES

Push two pins – about a centimetre apart – through a piece of thick card. Now touch the pin points gently against a finger tip. You can tell easily that there are indeed two pins.

Now touch the top of your back with the two pins. You will probably be able to feel only one pin.

Try touching other parts of your body with the pins to see how the sensitivity varies.

This happens because the nerve endings beneath the skin that respond to touch are closer together in some parts of the body. On the fingertips there are as many as a thousand touch nerves to every 6 square centimetres of skin.

Touch a friend's back with two pins. It is likely that they will have to be held some 5 centimetres apart before your friend realizes you are using two pins.

TASTE TEST Blindfold a friend and ask them to taste two different foods with a similar texture, for example a cube of uncooked potato and a cube of apple. Can they tell the difference? Do the same test but hold the taster's nose while they eat. Now hold a piece of onion under the taster's nose while they are eating a piece of apple. Ask them what they think they are eating.

VIBRATING EAR DRUM

Sound is caused by vibrations in the air. Inside the ear, at the end of the ear canal, is the ear drum. This also vibrates when sound waves hit it. You can make a drum vibrate in the same way.

Stretch a plastic sheet over the top of a big tin or bowl and hold it in place with an elastic band.

Sprinkle some sugar on the sheet.

Hit a metal tray near the drum and you will see the sugar bounce around on the plastic.

Hitting the tray causes the air around it to vibrate, and then vibrates the plastic, just like the membrane that forms your ear drum.

SEE YOUR PULSE

Carefully push a drawing pin into the bottom of a matchstick. Using the drawing pin as a stand, place the match at the base of your wrist.

The head of the match will vibrate with your pulse rate. The pulse rate of an average adult at rest is between 70 and 75 beats per minute. The pulse rate for a ten-year-old is about 90 beats a minute and for a baby about 140 beats per minute.

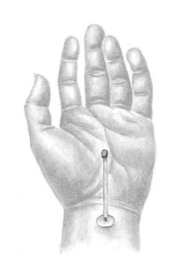

MOST INFECTIOUS DISEASE is pneumonic plague. Two or three plague bacilli will fatally infect test animals.

FIRST HUMAN HEART TRANSPLANT OPERATION was performed on Louis Washkansky at the Groote Schuur Hospital, Cape Town on 3 December, 1967 by Professor Christiaan Barnard.

FIRST FALSE TEETH. The first individual porcelain teeth were introduced by Giuseppangelo Fonzi in the early 19th century.

PENICILLIN. On 12 February, 1941 penicillin was used for the first time on a human patient. It had been discovered by Sir Alexander Fleming in September 1928. A few patients were treated with the new discovery but it was not until 1940 that Howard Florey and Ernest Chain discovered how to make pure penicillin in sufficient quantities for general use.

NASTY MEDICINE

Try these tricks to help nasty medicine go down.

Hold your nose as you take the medicine. Because our sense of taste is affected by the way things smell, you can cut down on the taste by holding your nose.

Suck a peppermint before taking the medicine. Peppermint is such a strong taste that it over-powers the taste of the medicine.

Suck an ice cube before taking the medicine. The ice freezes the taste buds for a little while so you will not taste the medicine so much.

Try all three methods together!

LISTEN TO YOUR HEART

First make a simple stethoscope. This consists of a length of rubber tubing attached to the bowl of a pipe.

Place the pipe bowl against your heart and hold the other end of the tube to your ear. The regular noises you hear are your heart beats.

First Aid is what it says it is – **first aid** – performed on the spot to help the patient until proper medical attention arrives. The best way to learn about first aid is to attend a course – perhaps one run by your local Red Cross. Here we show some of the basic principles of first aid.

UNCONSCIOUSNESS

A person who becomes unconscious should be turned on to his or her side as quickly as possible. If you are on your own pulling the patient's clothing at the hip will help.

2. Make sure the patient's head is on one side.

7. Make sure nothing is blocking the mouth, all tight clothing is loosened, and that the patient gets lots of air

3. Move the upper arm until it is bent to form a right angle to the rest of the body.

4. Move the lower arm backwards to lie alongside the patient's back.

5. Bend the upper leg upwards until it is in a position similar to that of the upper arm.

6. Straighten the under leg until it is only slightly bent.

TAKING THE PULSE

Place your fingers on the underside of the wrist.

Count the number of pulses in a minute. Normal pulse rate is about 70. If it is below 60 or above 80 call a doctor.

ARTIFICIAL RESPIRATION

This is necessary if someone has stopped breathing.

Remove any obstructions to breathing such as a tight tie etc.

Run your fingers around the inside of the person's mouth to check that the tongue is not blocking the air passages.

Support the patient at the back of the neck and tilt the head backwards with the chin pointing upward. In this position it is quite possible that the patient will begin breathing unaided. If not, go on to the next stage.

Open your mouth and take a deep breath. Hold the patient's nostrils together and then place your lips completely around the mouth. Blow into the mouth gently until you see the chest rise.

As you remove your mouth the chest should fall and you then continue the same process – blowing into the mouth and then coming away – at a normal breathing rate.

Continue until the patient starts breathing.

Between breaths shout for help.

IT IS A GOOD IDEA TO PRACTISE THIS TECHNIQUE BUT *NEVER, NEVER*, ON A HEALTHY PERSON. USE A DOLL OR A DUMMY FOR PRACTICE.

TREATING SHOCK

Treatment for shock should be given for every accident. But if the patient is injured, treat the injury first.

Until help arrives comfort the patient, and show calmly that you are in command of the situation.

The patient should lie down quietly. Loosen any restrictive clothing. If possible, the head of the patient should be slightly lower than the legs.

Keep the patient warm but do not apply artificial heat such as massage or hot water bottles.

The patient is likely to ask for a drink, but must not be given anything.

WOUNDS

No wound should be ignored.

If there is a lot of blood, try to raise the injured part higher than the rest of the body. A bleeding hand should be lifted in the air.

Serious bleeding should be stopped as soon as possible. First cover the wound with a clean dressing then press with the thumb or the palm of the hand while trying to hold the wound together.

If there is likely to be anything in the wound, press on the sides not directly on to the wound.

After applying pressure put clean bandages over the wound. Do not attempt a tourniquet.

BROKEN BONES: support the fractured bone by a cushion; move patient as little as possible; stop any bleeding and treat skin wounds. **If a leg is fractured**, do not move it. **If an arm is fractured**, gently bandage it against the body; lay injured person on a couch.

OTHER PROBLEMS

BURNS AND SCALDS: Plunge the affected part into cold water immediately. This will take the heat from the burn. Dry the area, being careful not to burst any blister that may have formed and put a dry dressing on it. If the burning or scalding is extensive, call a doctor.

STINGS: Treat wasp stings with vinegar; bee stings with bicarbonate of soda and hot water or mix some of the powder with cold water into a paste. Stings on the mouth require a doctor's attention.

BLISTERS: Do not burst the blister. The fluid in the blister protects the skin underneath. Cover the blister with a dry dressing and allow it to dry up naturally.

ANIMALS

The system used for the classification of living things was invented by the Swedish botanist Carl von Linné (1707–1778). His book *Species Plantarum*, (1753) gives the basic system of plant classification, and animal classification is described in his *Systema Naturae* (1758).

As Linne's books were written in Latin – the scientific language of the time – he is better known by his Latin name, Carolus Linnaeus. His system still forms the basis of modern classification.

THE SEVEN GROUPS

In Linnaeus' system there are seven main groups (taxa), in which every living thing is placed for identification. These are:

SPECIES: a group having common characteristics and capable of cross breeding to produce offspring of the same kind.

GENUS (plural: GENERA): a group of closely related species. Some genera consist of just one species.

FAMILY: a group of related genera.

ORDER: a group of allied families.

CLASS: a group of related orders.

PHYLUM (plural: PHYLA): a group of related classes.

KINGDOM: the largest group of all. There are two main kingdoms: the animal kingdom (Animalia); the plant kingdom (Plantae).

HUMAN CLASSIFICATION

KINGDOM	Animal	
PHYLUM	Chordata	animals with a backbone
CLASS	Mammalia	warm blooded animals that suckle their young
ORDER	Primate	the highest order of mammals
FAMILY	Hominidae	the family of Man
GENERA	Homo	human
SPECIES	sapiens	the wise

To mention every group when describing an organism would be cumbersome. Scientists normally use just the genus and species – Man, for example, is called Homo sapiens.

DARWIN'S FINCHES

Swedish naturalist Linnaeus (left) and British 'evolutionist' Darwin.

Some most unusual animals are to be found on the Galapagos Islands in the Pacific, 960 kilometres west of Ecuador. These islands and the creatures on them provided the main evidence for Charles Darwin's book *Origin of Species* which set out the theory of evolution (the belief that creatures change and adapt to make the best use of their environment).

Darwin came to his conclusions because the creatures on Galapagos had developed in their own way to make the best of the conditions in which they had to live. One of the most striking of the animals Darwin found was the giant tortoise, from which the islands take their name galapago, Spanish for 'tortoise'.

Also found in the Galapagos are iguanas. These lizards can grow up to 1.25 metres long.

Three of the 14 species of finches on the Galapagos Islands.

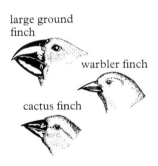

large ground finch

warbler finch

cactus finch

But it was from the finches that Darwin gained most evidence for his theories. There are some 14 species on the islands. All have descended from one, original, species but each one has adapted to a particular environment.

THE VERTEBRATES

The animal kingdom can be divided into two large groups: vertebrates (with backbones) and invertebrates (without backbones). Within each group other classifications allow us to group different species of animals. Here are the vertebrates:

MAMMALS

REPRODUCTION They give birth to live young which they suckle.
HABITAT Mainly on land; sometimes in water.
BREATHING Even water-dwelling mammals breathe air through lungs.

AMPHIBIANS

REPRODUCTION They lay shell-less eggs in water. The tadpoles undergo metamorphosis.
HABITAT Land and in water.
BREATHING The tadpoles breathe through gills; the adults through lungs.

BIRDS

REPRODUCTION They lay eggs which they hatch.
BODY PROTECTION Feathers.
HABITAT Land and in the air.
BREATHING They breathe air through lungs.
OTHER CHARACTERISTICS A beak and two wings.

REPTILES

REPRODUCTION They mostly lay eggs on land but do not hatch them.
HABITAT Land and/or water.
BREATHING They breathe air through lungs.
OTHER CHARACTERISTICS Some have four legs, others none at all.

FISH

REPRODUCTION They lay shell-less eggs in water, which they usually abandon.
HABITAT Water.
BREATHING They breathe through gills oxygen dissolved in water.

Rhinos are threatened with extinction.

Humans are responsible for a great deal of damage to the environment and this in turn has put many animals under threat. The dodo, the great auk, the Arabian ostrich, the Syrian wild ass, the Tasmanian emu and the South African blue buck are a few of over one hundred creatures that have become recently extinct.

Time is running out for many more species including the White rhino, cheetahs, the Arabian oryx and the Polar bear. As more areas are being cleared the habitats of many creatures and plants continue to disappear.

There are several international organizations fighting against this trend. They include the World Wildlife Fund and Greenpeace

AUSTRALIAN ANIMALS

When Australia became separated from the rest of Asia, to which it was once joined, the animal life evolved there in a unique way.

Perhaps the best known of these animals is the KANGAROO, the females of which carry their young in a pouch. Animals which have a pouch (*marsupium*) are called marsupials.

Another strange Australian creature is the

kangaroo

spiny anteater

ECHIDNA, or SPINY ANTEATER. This nocturnal creature is covered with spines.

Possibly the strangest of all animals, is the DUCK-BILLED PLATYPUS. Like a duck, it has a bill and webbed feet – but it has the fur-covered body of a mammal, lays eggs, like a bird, and suckles its young like a mammal. The platypus lives in rivers and is a good swimmer.

duck-billed platypus

LARGEST LAND ANIMAL

The Bush Elephant of Africa (*Loxodonta africana*) stands about 3.20 metres in height and weighs about 5.5 tonnes.

● There are two species of elephant: the African elephant and the Indian elephant.

The African elephant is larger and has bigger ears than the Indian elephant.

Both the male and the female African elephants have tusks; in the Indian elephant only the male has tusks.

At the end of its trunk the African elephant has two projections, or 'fingers'; the Indian has only one.

An African elephant has four toes on each of its front feet and three toes on its hind feet; the Indian elephant has five toes on its fore feet and four toes on its hind feet. The Indian elephant can be trained to move heavy loads.

● An elephant's ears are more important as a cooling system than for hearing. Elephants have bad hearing and poor eyesight but they have an excellent sense of smell.

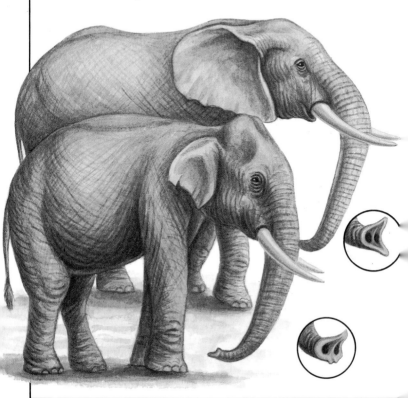

TALLEST ANIMAL

From their feet to the tip of their horns giraffes (*Giraffa camelopardalis*) measure about 5 metres. Giraffes were once quite common all over Africa south of the Sahara but hunting reduced their numbers drastically. They are now a protected species.

● The smallest non-flying mammal is the PYGMY SHREW (*Suncus etruscus*). It measures only 40 millimetres and has a tail of about 25 millimetres.

pygmy shrew

BUMBLEBEE BAT of Thailand is the smallest mammal in the world. The head and body measure just 35 millimetres and it has a wing span of 150 millimetres.

There are some 750 species of bats (*Chiroptera*). They are nocturnal creatures and they use an echo-location system to find their way in the dark.

● Fastest animals on land are CHEETAHS (*Acinonyx jubatus*). They can run at up to 96 km/h on level ground, but only for a short distance.

CLOSEST TO HUMANS

The gorilla is the largest member of the ape family. Although gorillas can stand two metres high, weigh 200 kilograms and appear ferocious, they are gentle creatures.

The gorilla comes from the rain forests of equatorial Africa but, like many other creatures, is now in danger of extinction from jungle clearance and from hunters.

The famous BARBARY APES on the rock of Gibraltar are really not apes at all but a species of Macaque monkey (*Macaca sylvana*) from India.

MAKE A PLASTER CAST

Choose a footprint that is well defined.

Put a strip of cardboard around the print. Secure the ends of the card with adhesive tape.

Press the bottom edge of the card down hard to be flat with the ground.

Mix some plaster of Paris in a bowl until it forms a creamy consistency. Pour the mixture into the cardboard surround to a depth of about 5 cm.

When the plaster has set you can remove the cardboard ring and lift the plaster. On the underside there will be a raised impression of the footprint.

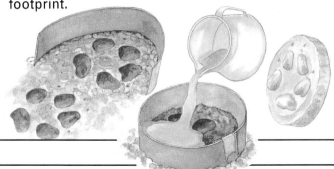

SMALLEST & FASTEST BIRD

The HELENA HUMMINGBIRD (*Mellisuga helenae*) measures only 58 mm from the tip of its beak to the end of its tail. Its eggs (11 by 8 mm) are the smallest egg laid by any bird. It lives in Cuba and the Isle of Pines.

With their wings beating some 90 times a second, hummingbirds are so active that it has been estimated they burn some 155,000 calories a day (human daily consumption is only 3500 calories!).

The PEREGRINE FALCON (above) can dive at over 300 km/h.

Every year millions of birds migrate. Some migratory flights are very long indeed. There are many theories of how birds navigate. It is likely that they use landmarks, the position of the Sun and the stars, and the Earth's magnetic field.

LONGEST SNAKE

The longest snake is the RETICULATED PYTHON (*Python reticulatus*) of

south-east Asia. It can measure more than 6 metres – there is even a record of one being as long as 10 metres!

The THREAD SNAKE is only about 100 mm long. As well as being the shortest snake it is also very rare. It is found only on the islands of Martinique, Barbados and St. Lucia.

The Blue Whale (*Balaenoptera musculus*) is usually between 20 and 26 metres long and weighs between 55 and 100 tonnes. One Blue Whale caught in the early 1900s measured 33.58 metres!

At the beginning of this century there were some 210,000 Blue Whales in the oceans but there are now only about 6,000.

● Vietnamese fishermen used to regard whales as messengers of the god of the sea. Anyone who found a dead whale or dolphin went into mourning for three months.

● There are two groups of whale: Baleen whales (*Mysticeti*) and the more common Toothed whales (*Odontoceti*). Baleen whales have a curtain of stiff, hairy material (called 'baleen') in their mouths which is used to filter krill from the water. The largest of the Toothed whales is the Sperm whale which has the largest brain of any creature in the world. This group also includes dolphins and porpoises.

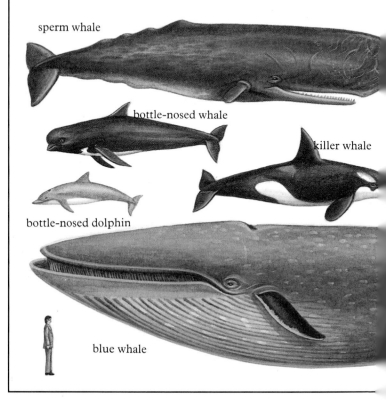

sperm whale

bottle-nosed whale

killer whale

bottle-nosed dolphin

blue whale

It takes ten tonnes of plankton to feed one tonne of krill (small shrimp-like creatures). A large whale eats a tonne of krill each day.

Whales are threatened with extinction because they are being killed faster than they can breed. Whales have only one enemy – humans.

● A whale's body is covered with blubber which can be up to 30 centimetres thick depending upon the species. Blubber contains oil. It is for this oil, and for their meat, that whales are hunted.

ESTIMATED NUMBER OF WHALES

Name	1900	Now
Blue	210,000	6,000
Humpback	100,000	6,000
Right	50,000	4,000
Bowhead	10,000	2,000
Fin	450,000	100,000
Sei	200,000	50,000

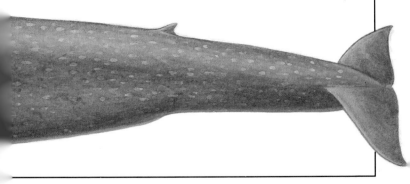

More than half a bird's weight is in its muscles and the largest muscles are those that work the wings.

Birds' beaks and claws are adapted for special purposes – webbed feet for swimming and beaks designed for cracking, scooping, tearing etc.

There may be as many as 1,500 million RED-BILLED QUELA (*Quela quela*) in Africa, making it the most abundant species of bird in the world. Its nickname is 'the feathered locust' because it destroys cereal crops.

The HORNBILL is a most mysterious bird. It has a crest on its bill, large eyelashes, walls itself into a hole in a tree when having young, and its wings make a loud noise in flight.

Hornbill

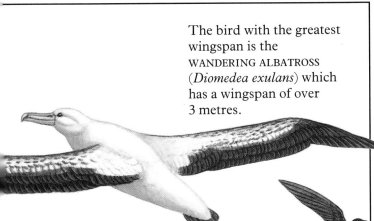

The bird with the greatest wingspan is the WANDERING ALBATROSS (*Diomedea exulans*) which has a wingspan of over 3 metres.

The SPINE-TAILED SWIFT of Asia can fly faster than any other bird and has been recorded at a speed of well over 150 km/h.

FLIGHTLESS BIRDS

Not all birds can fly. The best known flightless birds are PENGUINS. There are about 18 species and all live in the southern half of the world. The largest is the Emperor Penguin which stands about a metre high.

There are several species of flightless birds in New Zealand. The best known is the KIWI. It is so short-sighted that it cannot see much farther than the end of its long, curved beak. It comes out at night to feed, using its long beak with sensitive nostrils at its tip (a feature found in no other bird) to smell and dig out earthworms and insects.

The NORTH AFRICAN OSTRICH (*Struthio camelus*) is another flightless bird. It stands at up to 2.75 metres and weighs up to 156.6 kilograms. It is the largest of all living birds. It also lays the largest egg of any bird.

A kiwi

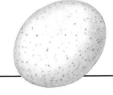

BIRDWATCHING

Birdwatching need cost you nothing. You can watch birds in your own garden, in streets, parks, the country and at the coast. A pair of binoculars are worth having and it is a good idea to buy a book to help you identify the various species.

Put out food for birds to help them through periods of bad weather and to attract them to your garden. If you put food on the ground it may also attract cats, dogs and other animals, so make a simple bird-table. It could be just a shallow box attached to the top of a pole driven into the ground. How to make a more complicated table is shown on the opposite page.

You could also make a nesting box (opposite). Remember that the base of the box should be at least 10 cm square and the hole should be at least 12 cm from the floor. Make sure the box is out of reach of cats and in a position where it doesn't face into the sun or bad weather.

swallow

house martin

sand martin

wren

bluetit

dunnock

robin

tree sparrow

pied wagtail

chaffinch

blackbird

song thrush

starli

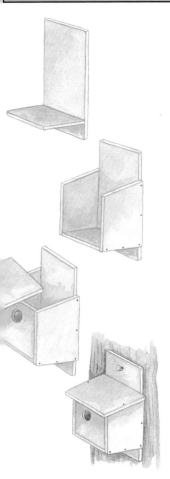

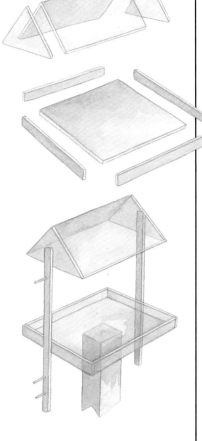

WATER FOUNTAIN

Fill a jar with water. Place a shallow dish over the top of the jar and then turn the whole lot upside down. Pour some water into the shallow dish.

Lift the jar just enough for you to push two or three small tin lids under its rim.

Place the water fountain on your bird-table and the dish will fill automatically as the birds drink from it.

There are a million different types of insect. The body of an insect consists of three parts: the head, the thorax, and the abdomen. There are usually a pair of feelers, called antennae, on the head. If the insect has wings, these and the legs are attached to the thorax.

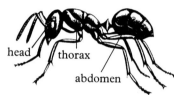

head thorax abdomen

Insects can live from 17 days, in the case of the male common house fly, up to the 50 years of queen termites. Some scientists believe that queen termites can live as long as a hundred years.

There are about 4000 different species of LADYBIRD. They vary in colour and number of spots.

Voracious eaters of aphids, they are popular with fruit growers and gardeners. Fifteenth-century farmers were so pleased with the work done by the ladybird that they petitioned the Pope to give it some special recognition. The Pope dedicated the insect to the Virgin Mary and called it the 'Beetle of Our Lady'.

The TROPICAL STICK INSECT (*Pharnacia serratipes*), from Indonesia, is the largest of the world's insects. Its head and body can measure up to 300 mm and the overall length can be almost double that.

LARGEST BUTTERFLY: Average wing-spans of between 203 and 228 mm belong to the Queen Alexandra birdwing butterfly of New Guinea.

LARGEST MOTH: There are two contenders for the title. They are the Hercules emperor moth (*Cosdinoscera hercules*) which lives in tropical Australia and New Guinea, and the great owlet moth (*Thysania agrippina*) of Central America. They have wing-spans of between 267 mm and 360 mm.

SMALLEST BUTTERFLY: *Micropsyche ariana*, of Afghanistan has a wing-span of only 7 mm. The world's SMALLEST MOTH, *Stigmella ridiculosa*, found in the Canary Islands has a wing-span of only 2 mm!

SOME BUTTERFLIES AND MOTHS

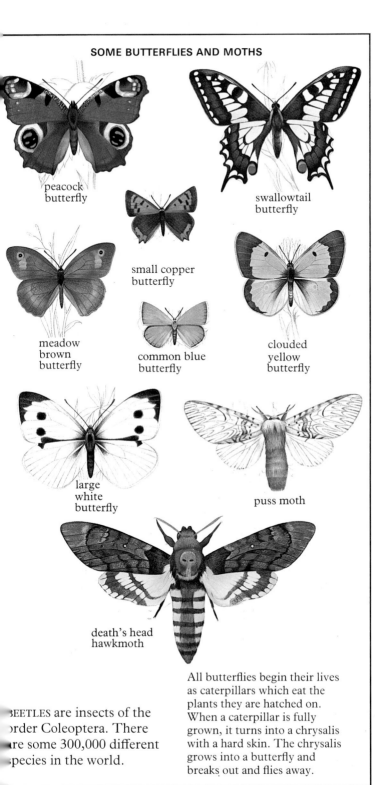

peacock
butterfly

swallowtail
butterfly

small copper
butterfly

meadow
brown
butterfly

common blue
butterfly

clouded
yellow
butterfly

large
white
butterfly

puss moth

death's head
hawkmoth

BEETLES are insects of the order Coleoptera. There are some 300,000 different species in the world.

All butterflies begin their lives as caterpillars which eat the plants they are hatched on. When a caterpillar is fully grown, it turns into a chrysalis with a hard skin. The chrysalis grows into a butterfly and breaks out and flies away.

There are at least 15,000 species of ANT around the world varying in size from 3 millimetres up to 35 millimetres for the female alligator ant of the Amazon. It has been estimated that there are some 10,000 billion ants in the world.

● When a BEE returns to the hive with nectar it performs a strange dance-like movement. The sequences in this dance tell the other bees where nectar is to be found.

If the dance is in the form of a fast circle the other bees know the nectar source is quite near. Should the returning bee cut through the circle and wriggle its abdomen as it dances this indicates that the flowers are over 100 metres away. The various directions in which the bee dances indicate the direction in relation to the Sun.

In sunny weather a hive of bees can make a kilogram of honey a day. This means visiting some 100,000 flowers to gather nectar.

AN ANT'S TRAIL

As ants go searching for food they leave a scent trail that other ants can follow.

See such a trail in action by putting some sugar or honey on a large sheet of paper and place it near an ants' nest. One ant will discover the food and it will not be long before the others follow.

Now move the food to another part of the paper. Most of the ants will follow the original trail to where the food was at the start before proceeding to its new location.

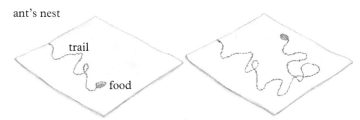

ant's nest

trail

food

Cutaway section shows a fish's gills

RECORDS

Even though fish are streamlined to enable them to move through water quickly they move much slower than land animals. The fastest fish is the COSMOPOLITAN SAILFISH (*Istiophorus platypterus*), capable of a speed of 109 km/h over short distances!

Fish use three methods of swimming:
  Muscular movements of the whole body.
  Fin and tail movements.
  Propulsion of water from the gills.

Fish and many other water creatures breathe by means of gills. Water is taken in through the mouth and passes over the gills which absorb oxygen from the water and get rid of carbon dioxide.

A microscope is needed to examine the world's smallest fish – for the longest example is only 10 mm long. The fish is the colourless and almost transparent DWARF GOBY (*Trimmatom nanus*) of the central Indian Ocean.

The world's largest fish, the WHALE SHARK (*Rhincodon typus*), is found in the warm areas of the Atlantic. Although it lives on plankton (small animals and plants on the ocean surface), it measures over five metres from head to tail.

The legs of the JAPANESE SPIDER CRAB (*Macrocheira kaempferi*) stretch to more than three metres.

- There are some fish that can survive out of water. The MUDSKIPPER has specially adapted fins that enable it to walk on dry land in search of food. During the dry season the Lung Fish of Africa can remain underground for long periods.

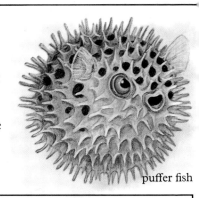
puffer fish

A GREAT DELICACY

In Japan a great delicacy called fugu is made from the Japanese puffer fish, the most poisonous fish in the world! In spite of the great care taken by chefs in preparing the dish several people die in Japan each year after eating fugu. There is no known antidote.

The porcupine fish, like the puffer fish, blows itself up like a balloon when attacked. Its body is covered with sharp spines to deter any predator from eating it.

UGLIEST FISH

What must be the ugliest fish are the various species of ANGLER FISH. It has a crafty way of catching its food. On top of its head is an imitation worm. This is wriggled until another fish tries to catch it, whereupon the Angler makes its attack.

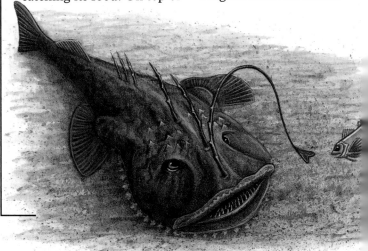

PETS

Before buying any pet make certain you can provide the food, love, care, exercise and attention it will need. Also be sure you can afford it as some pets can prove expensive to keep. You may have to pay vet's bills for injections for a young kitten or puppy. Find out all you can about the pet you want before actually getting it.

The choice of pet is wide – cats, dogs, mice, birds, gerbils, hamsters, fish, rabbits.

DOGS

Dogs make excellent companions. You have a huge number of different breeds to choose from. **DO NOT** buy a puppy without giving it a lot of careful thought. Remember that puppies grow up and a big dog will need a lot of exercise. The heaviest breeds are the St Bernard and the Old English Mastiff, both of which can weigh up to 91 kilograms. At the opposite end of the weight scale are the Chihuahua, Toy poodle and Yorkshire Terrier.

● Dogs live from between 8 and 15 years. This should be taken into consideration when choosing a dog as a pet. Your puppy will need a comfortable basket, a collar and lead and a feeding bowl. You must take advice on what to feed your puppy and how often – a young puppy may need four or five small meals a day. Always make sure it has plenty of fresh water.

Your puppy will probably not be house trained. You will need to be patient and firm and make it obey you.

CATS

Cats need freedom to come and go as they please. There are many breeds of domestic cats.

At first your kitten will need five meals a day, one being a milk feed. A tablespoonful of food each time is enough. As the kitten grows, cut down the meals to three bigger feeds and then, when it is six months, to two

At first your kitten will need a litter tray, but when it has settled in, it should

be trained to go in the garden. To save you the trouble of letting it in and out, put a cat flap in the back door. Your cat will soon learn to use it.

It must also be taken to the vet to be inoculated against a killer illness called feline infectious enteritis. A carrying box is useful for taking it there and on any other journeys.

BIRDS

Before you can teach a budgerigar to talk you must train it to come onto your finger. Put your hand into its cage gently and keep doing this until it is no longer afraid of you. The next stage is to tickle

the bird's breast gently. When the bird allows you to do this place your finger near its feet so the bird can step on it.

Repeat the bird's name continuously until the bird imitates you.

RABBITS

RABBITS need a roomy, draught-free and dry hutch. It should be cleaned at least once a week. You can buy special rabbit food from a pet shop. Feed your

rabbit twice a day and add treats such as dandelion leaves or a carrot. Change water regularly. Does usually make better pets than bucks.

HOW TO PICK UP A RABBIT

Never pick a rabbit up by its ears as this can be painful. You should lift a rabbit by first grasping the skin at the back of its neck. You should then place your other hand under its body to give it support.

HORSE TALK

Owning a horse is to many a dream. But there are times when you will come across a horse or pony and you should know how to pat or feed it safely. The first rule is never enter a field or stable without the owner's permission. And never stand behind a horse or run up to it. It could kick. If a horse's ears point forward, it is interested in you and you need not be afraid to go closer. If its ears are flat back, it is in a bad mood. Stroke a horse's muzzle and pat its neck gently. Stand slightly to one side so it can see you better. Offer it largish pieces of dry bread, or carrot or apple from the flat palm of your hand. Scratch between the ears and under the mane, talking softly all the time. You can offer a horse freshly picked grass (not grass clippings). Most horses love mints. Many horses become friendly if you breathe heavily through your nostrils!

PET BOTTLE

Never give small animals such as mice or hamsters water in an ordinary dish. They will foul the water with their droppings and may tip the dish over so making the cage damp and unhealthy.

Special water bottles can be bought from pet shops but it is also very easy to make your own. You will need a small bottle, a rubber cork with a hole in it, and an angled piece of glass tubing.

Push the tubing through the hole in the cork. Fill the bottle, push in the cork and clip the bottle to the side of the cage with the end of the tubing inside the cage. A suitable clip can be obtained from your pet shop.

FORESTS

What role does a forest play?

- It prevents erosion
- acts on the climate
- provides oxygen
- is home for countless animals

Enemies of the forest.

- Humans who over-exploit;
- humans who do not renew felled areas;
- fire which destroys thousands of hectares a year;
- insect damage.

A thousand hectares of forest will each day produce between 300 and 1000 litres of oxygen.

A BRISTLECONE PINE (*Pinus longaeva*) on Wheeler Peak, Nevada, USA, has been named 'Methuselah'. It is reckoned to be 4600 years old.

COAST REDWOODS (*Sequoia sempervirens*) are the tallest trees in the world. The 'Harry Cole' tree, in Humboldt Redwoods State Park, California, towers over 112 metres.

A MONTEZUMA CYPRESS in Mexico with a diameter of 12 metres is the tree with the thickest trunk.

Two main groups of trees: deciduous and coniferous.

You can tell the age of a tree by counting the number of rings in a cross-section of the trunk. Each year a new layer of cells is added to the trunk, just below the bark. Experts can even tell what the weather was like in particular years by studying tree rings.

Every day humans destroy large areas of trees. In the past 30 years over half of the world's woodlands and forests have disappeared.

This is having a terrible effect on life on this planet. Without trees erosion begins to take place. Rain does not go into the soil but simply washes away. Trees provide the atmosphere with oxygen and water vapour – both of which are vital to life. Trees absorb carbon dioxide which is one of the gases causing global warming. So climate is affected by trees and the world is heating up partly because of the increased felling of trees. The long-term effects of this could be disastrous for our planet.

HOW HIGH IS THAT TREE?

From a piece of thick card cut out a right-angled triangle. (The two sides that form the right angle must be the same length.)

Make a small hole near the centre. Draw a line from the hole down to one of the shorter edges, parallel to the other short edge. Tie a string through the hole. To the other end of the string attach a small weight. When the string is over the drawn line you are holding the triangle straight.

Look along the long edge of the triangle to the top of the tree. Now walk backwards or forwards, still looking at the top of the tree, until the plumb line is absolutely vertical.

Measure the distance from where you stand to the tree. That, plus your height, is the tree's height.

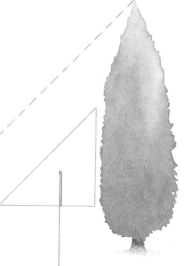

HOW SEEDS TRAVEL

The seeds of some plants are blown about by the wind. Wind dispersed plants include the dandelion, the seeds of which have tiny fluffy 'parachutes' attached to them. The seeds of a poppy are held in a seed case and shaken free by the wind. Some, like the sycamore, have special 'wings'.

The seeds of many plants have hooks, or burrs. A passing animal picks up some of these hooked seeds in its fur.

Many seeds are dispersed by an exploding seed pod. When the seeds are ready, the pod bursts open and the seeds are scattered. Violets have seed pods that go pop.

Birds scatter seeds simply by eating the fruit. The seeds pass through their disgestive system.

Rivers and seas carry the seeds of some plants from place to place. Coconuts are an example of this.

SPROUT A SALAD
Put a handful of green mung beans in a jar. Cover the top of the jar with a piece of muslin.

Pour water into the jar, through the cloth, then pour the water out again.

Lay the jar on its side and leave it in a warm, dark place. Water each day. Soon your jar will be full of lovely, crunchy beansprouts.

PLANT A PINEAPPLE

To grow a plant from a pineapple top, dip it first in some rooting powder.

Put the pineapple top in a pot of peat from your garden shop. The peat should come half way up the sides of the pineapple. Keep the pot in a light, warm place. Water often.

It will not be long before the plant begins to develop leaves. If you are lucky, you may even have a pineapple growing on your plant.

MULTI-COLOURED FLOWER

Mix some red ink in a glass of water and some blue ink in another glass of water.

Split the stem of a white flower, such as a rose, or a carnation. Place one half of the stalk in the red liquid and the other in the blue.

After a few hours you will have a flower that is half one colour and half the other. The inks are conveyed up the fine tubes in the stem which carry food to the plant.

CRYSTALIZED ROSE PETALS
Dip the petals in beaten egg white and then lay them on greaseproof paper which has been covered with castor sugar. Sprinkle more sugar over the petals and leave them to dry and crystalize.

BOTTLE GARDEN

You will need: a large plastic lemonade bottle; sharp knife; glue (suitable for use with plastic); small stones; soil; and a few small house plants.

Remove the black base from the bottle. Cut the bottom from the bottle and then cut the top off. Keep the cap on.

Turn the base upside down and glue it to the bottom of the bottle. Put some stones in the bottom and then fill it with soil.

Put in the plants and give them a small quantity of water.

Glue the top of the bottle onto the base and your bottle garden is complete. It needs no watering.

BOTTLED FRUIT

If you have an apple tree in your garden you can try this amazing bottled fruit.

When the fruit on the tree is very small place a narrow necked bottle over it. Use string to tie the bottle to the branch. The apple will continue to grow on the tree – but inside the bottle.

Eventually the apple will grow so big it is impossible to get it out of the bottle.

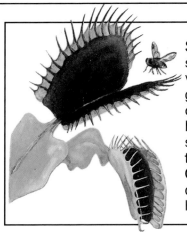

Some plants feed on small insects. The VENUS FLY-TRAP which grows in marshy areas of South Carolina has hinged leaves which snap fast on any insect that dares land on it. Once the plant has digested its prey the leaves open again.

RARE FLOWERING

The UMBRELLA BAMBOO (*Thamnocalamus spathaceus*) flowers just once every hundred years. It was discovered in the 1880s by Dr Augustine Henry, and Irish botanist, and Guillaume Farges, a French priest who were travelling in China and were lucky enough to see it in bloom. All the umbrella bamboos in cultivation have derived from a single plant sent from China in 1910.

LEAF PRESERVATION

In the spring pick a twig with some young leaves on it. Split the end of the twig and strip off about 5 centimetres of bark.

In a jar mix one part of glycerine to two parts of warm water. Stand the twig in the jar, covering the area of stripped bark. Leave the twig standing in the liquid for at least a week.

SCIENCE AND TECHNOLOGY

SOME OUTSTANDING SCIENTISTS

ARCHIMEDES (287–212 BC, Greek). Founder of the science of hydrostatics.

CURIE, MARIE (1867–1934, Polish) and her husband PIERRE (1859–1906, French) discovered the radioactive element radium.

ALBERT EINSTEIN (1879–1955, German). His *General Theory of Relativity* caused scientists to alter their view of gravitation.

MICHAEL FARADAY (1791–1867, British) discovered the principles of electro-magnetism.

GALILEO (1564–1642, Italian) discovered the laws of pendulums and falling bodies.

SIR ISAAC NEWTON (1642–1727, English). In his book *Principia* (1687) he recorded his amazing discoveries of the laws of motion and the theories of gravitation.

ERNEST (LORD) RUTHERFORD (1871–1937, New Zealander) developed the modern nuclear theory.

HOW TO WEIGH AIR Tie a piece of string to the middle of a long stick so that the stick remains level when you hold the string. Now tie an inflated balloon to each end of the stick. Slide the balloon strings along the stick until the stick hangs level.

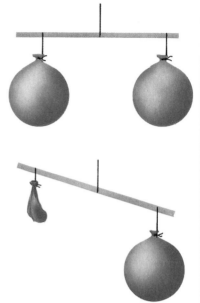

Burst one of the balloons and the end of the stick with the inflated balloon will tilt downwards. The weight of the air pulls it down. Burst the second balloon and the stick will level again.

Push two sink plungers together as hard as you can. Now try to pull them apart – it is very difficult.

This is because you have removed most of the air from the rubber cups. The air pressure on the outside of the cups is greater than that inside them so the outside air holds them together. This is known as the MAGDEBURG EXPERIMENT, after the German town where Otto von Guericke first performed the experiment in 1654 using iron spheres and two teams of horses to pull them apart.

● Without air no life is possible. A candle will no longer burn and a flower will wilt and die after they have used up the air in a jar covering them. Without air sound cannot be heard.

FIRE

Fire exists in the natural state in many places. From the fissured surface of the Earth comes fiery material. Volcanoes frequently throw up fiery magma and sometimes cause enormous damage. Lava can reach temperatures of over 1000°C.

Making fire with a bow drill.

- Fire is one of the great discoveries. About 750,000 years ago humans learned how to use fire which has been with us ever since. Thanks to it we can keep ourselves warm, cook our food, melt metals, illuminate our houses.

- What is combustion? Combustibles can be solids, liquids or gases. To burn, a combustible needs oxygen and in exchange it gives off carbon dioxide gas and water.

- Flames are different colours according to the combustible; the bluer the flame the hotter it is. A yellow flame is less hot and contains matter that will not burn, given off as smoke.

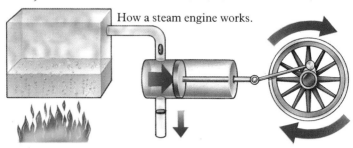

How a steam engine works.

DON'TS

Don't light a fire in a wood.
Do not open a container of inflammable material near a naked flame.
If you smell a gas leak don't strike a light.
If your clothes catch fire, do not run.

WATER

Water makes up three-quarters of the Earth's surface. Water is vital to life. Even our body is made up of 61% water. (46 kilograms for an adult weighing 70 kilograms!).

What does a litre of water weigh? One kilogram.

Water turns into ice at 0°Celsius.

Water can be used as a source of power – as in watermills.

NEWTON'S BOAT:
In 1687 Sir Isaac Newton published the *Principia*. In it he set out the laws of motion. One of these states that for every action there is an opposite and equal reaction.

Pour a little oil or washing-up liquid into the hole in the centre of a boat-shaped card. The oil would normally spread out across the surface of the water but the card stops it. It is forced to go along the narrow slit towards the rear of the boat. The force of the oil coming out from the boat causes the boat to move forward.

MATCH SPREAD

Gently arrange five matches in a bowl of water in the shape of a star.

Touch the water at the centre of the star with a small piece of soap, without disturbing the water.

The matches will move towards the edges of the bowl.

The water is pulling the matches with equal force on all sides. This force is called surface tension. The soap reduces the surface tension at the centre of the star and the stronger tension of the unsoaped water pulls the matches to the edge.

SPINNING COLOURS Cut a circle, with a radius of 5 cm, from a piece of stiff card. Colour one side with the colours exactly as shown.

Push a pencil through the centre of the card and then spin the card like a top. The card will appear white. This shows that light is made up of different colours.

MONEY MAGIC Light bends when it travels from the air to something transparent. This bending of light is called *refraction*.

You can see how refraction works if you place a stick in a large bowl of water. The stick will appear to bend.

In another experiment place a coin in a mug and then move back to a position where you cannot see the coin. Pour water into the mug and the coin will come into view because the water bends the light.

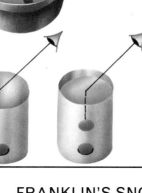

FRANKLIN'S SNOW EXPERIMENT

The American statesman Benjamin Franklin (1706–1790) tried many experiments of different types. Here is one you can try for yourself.

On a snowy day place two pieces of cloth, one white and one black, on top of the snow. Leave them there for several hours. You should now see a difference in the snow under each cloth. The snow beneath the dark cloth will have melted much more than that under the white cloth. This is because dark colours absorb the Sun's heat and light colours reflect it.

HOW TO GROW CRYSTALS

Many substances, such as sand, sugar, precious stones and salt are formed from crystals. In this experiment you can make some crystals.

Pour some very hot water into a clean pyrex bowl.

Stir several spoonfuls of washing soda or table salt into the bowl until all the mineral has dissolved. Keep adding spoonfuls of soda until no more will dissolve.

Tie a paper clip or a nail on one end of a piece of cotton. Tie the other end to a pencil. Now support the pencil over the bowl so the clip hangs in the water.

Leave the bowl undisturbed for a few days and crystals will form on the clip.

To make coloured crystals add some ink or poster paint to the water or use copper sulphate crystals.

STATIONARY COIN

Close your hand into a fist. Balance a sheet of card on the back of your hand and place a coin on it.

With your other hand flick the card away quickly. The card will fly off your hand but the coin will stay.

This is because everything has inertia, which means that it needs a force to make it move. Flicking the card provides enough force to make the card leave your hand but very little of that force is passed to the coin – so it remains where it is.

THE WHEEL Possibly the most important invention of prehistoric times was the wheel. It is often regarded as the most important invention ever made. The first wheels may have been simply tree trunks used as rollers.

Wheels made it possible to carry heavy loads over long distances and this helped increase trading between different places. Meetings between people of different communities led to a spread of ideas and the growth of civilization.

HOW STRONG ARE YOU?

After watching some slaves moving blocks of stone with poles Archimedes formulated the mathematical principles of leverage. He said that if he could stand in the correct place he would be able to move the world with just a lever.

The principles of leverage can be demonstrated with the help of two or four of your friends. You will need two broomsticks and a length of rope. Tie one end of the rope to one end of a broomstick and then wind the rope around both broomsticks as shown.

Ask your friends to try and keep the brooms apart while you try and pull them together. You should find that you are easily able to beat the pulling power of your friends.

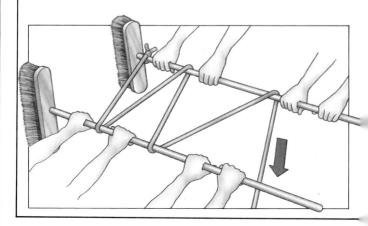

THE GENIUS OF DA VINCI

Leonardo (above left) designed some amazing machines, such as this multi-barrelled gun. He was also one of the most famous painters of the Renaissance. On the left is a detail from his *Virgin and St Anne*.

ARCHIMEDEAN SCREW
Early in the history of agriculture it became necessary to lift water up to higher ground levels. The greatest advance came when the mathematician Archimedes (c.287–212 BC) invented the Archimedean Screw (below).

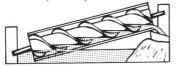

Leonardo da Vinci was a genius at inventing. He was born in 1452, too far ahead of his time. Many of the things he dreamed of did not become realities until this century.

In the 7000 pages of his notebooks are designs for helicopters, tanks, gas masks, an unsinkable ship, and a diving suit.

He also designed armoured vehicles, a dredger, a rope-making machine, a water clock, flying machines, and musical instruments. Leonardo is also one of the world's greatest artists.

PERPETUAL MOTION

People have long tried to devise a machine that would work without any external energy and which would keep on working for ever.

The laws of physics state that perpetual motion is impossible, yet inventors persist in trying to make a perpetual motion machine.

If such a machine were invented, it would answer all the world's energy problems.

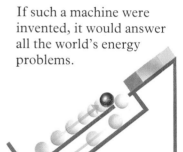

'Perpetual motion' machines.

NOBEL PRIZES

Alfred Nobel (1833–1896), the Swedish inventor of dynamite also instituted the Nobel Prizes. Nobel's father owned a business manufacturing nitro-glycerine, a highly explosive substance. In 1867 Alfred Nobel discovered a way to make it safer by impregnating it with sticks of Fuller's earth: dynamite.

Nobel made several other discoveries in the field of explosives but the fact that all his inventions could be used for war worried him. When he died he left 96% of his vast fortune to set up a foundation to award annual prizes for discoveries and excellence in the fields of peace, literature, science, physics and medicine.

The first programmable digital computer was designed by Charles Babbage in 1834. But his 'Analytical Engine' was never built – it was too advanced for Victorian engineering.

Various machines were built in later years but they were more like calculators than computers. The first true electronic computer was the ENIAC (Electronic Numerical Integrator and Calculator) built at the University of Pennsylvania in 1945. Soon computers became used widely in offices, but they were extremely large. When the silicon chip appeared in 1965 computers began to get smaller and the personal computer came into use.

INVENTED BY MISTAKE

In 1838 Louis Daguerre put an under-exposed photographic plate in a cupboard. When he went back the plate had been developed because of a forgotten saucer of mercury also in the cupboard. This mistake enabled Daguerre to speed up the developing of photographs.

Sir Alexander Fleming left some sample test jars open in his lab at St Mary's Hospital, London by mistake in 1928. Later he discovered the bacteria on one of them had been attacked by a spore that had settled on it. This led him to undertake more experiments. As a result, he discovered penicillin.

TALL STOREYS

Some 30,000 people work in the twin towers of the World Trade Center in New York. The towers are 411.5 metres high and there are 110 storeys, 43,600 windows and 234 lifts.

But the World Trade Center is not the world's tallest office building. That honour belongs to the 443-metre high Sears Tower in Chicago (475 metres with television antennae).

The world's tallest self-supporting structure is the 555-metre high CN Tower in Toronto. There are four glass-fronted lifts which carry people up to the revolving restaurant 347 metres above the ground.

There are television and radio towers taller than the CN Tower but they are supported by guy wires. The tallest – an amazing 646 metres – is the Warszawa Radio mast in Poland.

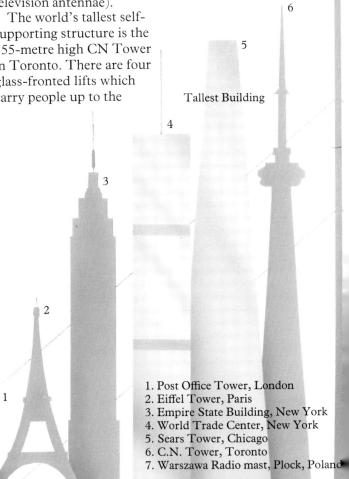

Tallest Building

1. Post Office Tower, London
2. Eiffel Tower, Paris
3. Empire State Building, New York
4. World Trade Center, New York
5. Sears Tower, Chicago
6. C.N. Tower, Toronto
7. Warszawa Radio mast, Plock, Poland

86

will be vertical. If it is hanging either towards or away from the door frame then the frame is not straight.

IS IT STRAIGHT?

Make a plumb line by tying a heavy weight to one end of two metres of string.

Now pin the line with a drawing pin to the top of a door frame, for example. When the weight has stopped swinging the line

IS IT LEVEL?

Make a spirit level by putting a strip of adhesive tape around an empty jar, about 5 cm parallel from the bottom.

Pour water into the jar until it is just below the tape and place the jar on a table. If the water level is parallel to the tape then the surface is level.

BUILD AN IGLOO

You need snow and skill.

Roll a snowball in the snow until it becomes sausage-shaped and about 25 cm in diameter. Place several of these rolls in a circle on the ground. This is the first layer of the igloo wall. (Leave a gap for the door!)

Put a second layer of snow rolls on top of the first and smooth the edges so the rolls stick together.

Continue building the wall until it is about a metre high. From now on each successive layer should overhang on the inside by about 5 cm.

Plug the hole in the roof with a roll pushed in endways. (And let an adult know what you are doing.)

LONGEST TUNNELS

The world's longest tunnel is the water supply tunnel which runs for 169 km from New York City to West Delaware in America.

The longest tunnel to carry traffic is the Seikan Rail Tunnel which runs under the sea of Tsugaru Strait between the Japanese islands of Honshu and Hokkaido. It is 53.85 km in length, just four kilometres more than the Channel Tunnel that is being constructed between England and France.

THE CHANNEL TUNNEL

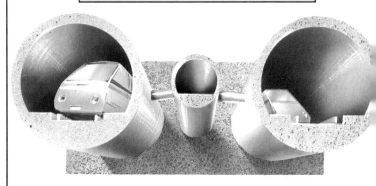

The Channel Tunnel, joining England and France, is expected to be open in May, 1993 (for some a dream come true).

There will be three tunnels: Two, each with a diameter of eight metres, for trains; and a service tunnel with a diameter of about five metres.

Tunnel length: 49.4 km, 38 km of which will be under the sea.

● **The first iron bridge** was built at Coalbrookdale, Shropshire by Abraham Darby in 1779. This arch bridge, with a span of 30 metres, now forms part of the Ironbridge Gorge open air museum.

● **The Great Wall of China** is the only man-made structure on Earth that is visible from the Moon. The emperor Shih Huang Ti started building it in the 3rd century BC to keep out the Tartars of central Asia. It stretches for over 2,400 kilometres.

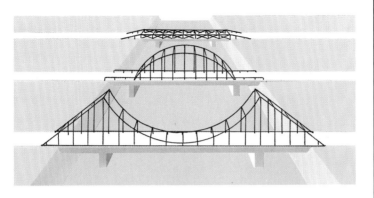

BRIDGE THAT GAP

There are three basic types of bridge: BEAM, ARCH or SUSPENSION.

The BASIC BEAM BRIDGE is simply a beam of steel supported on each bank. Longer beam bridges have to have supports at intervals across the span.

An ARCH BRIDGE is formed of one or several arches. This design is capable of bearing a greater weight than the beam design.

The main part of a SUSPENSION BRIDGE is a beam but this is supported by steel cables suspended from towers.

● **The longest single-span bridge** is the Humber Suspension Bridge across the estuary of the River Humber in England.

The main span is 1410 metres long but the complete bridge runs for 2220 metres.

FIRSTS OF THE ROAD

- STEAM-POWERED road vehicle was built by Nicolas Cugnot of France in about 1770. It was a three-wheel tractor.
- GAS-DRIVEN road vehicle was first built by Etienne Lenoir of France. In about 1863 it travelled about 10 kilometres in two hours.
- DIESEL-ENGINED vehicle, invented by Rudolf Diesel in 1897, exploded, nearly killing him.
- FIRST CARS sold to the public were German, made by Karl Benz in 1885.

- CHEAP CARS were pioneered by Henry Ford in the United States. Ford mass-produced 15,007,033 of his 'Tin Lizzie' between 1908 and 1927.
- THE FIRST TRAFFIC LIGHTS were set up in Detroit (USA) in 1919.
- In 1924 the world's first MOTORWAY was opened – from Milan to Varese in Italy.
- WHITE LINES running down the middle of the road were first used in Britain, in 1927.

first Daimler

steam-powered vehicle

Ford Tin Lizzie

Volkswagen Beetle

modern car

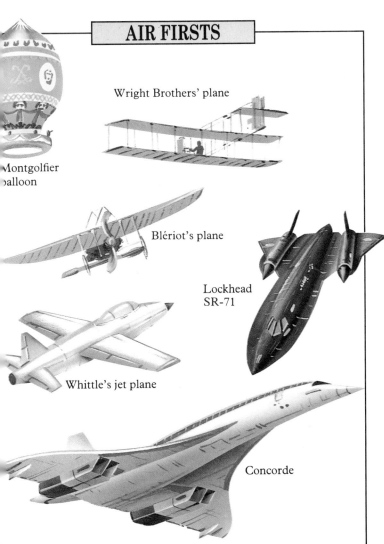

Wright Brothers' plane

Montgolfier balloon

Blériot's plane

Lockhead SR-71

Whittle's jet plane

Concorde

● FIRST MANNED BALLOON FLIGHT was made by Pilâtre de Rozier and the Marquis d'Arlandes over Paris in 1783.

● FIRST MANNED AEROPLANE FLIGHT was made by Orville Wright at Kitty Hawk, N. Carolina, USA, in 1903. His airborne journey lasted 12 seconds at an airspeed of 48 km/h. The plane had a 4-cylinder, 12 h.p. engine.

● FIRST INTERNATIONAL AIRPLANE FLIGHT was made by the French inventor Louis Blériot in 1909. He flew the 37.8 km across the Channel in 37 minutes.

● FIRST JET-PLANE ENGINE was patented by Frank Whittle of Britain in 1930.

● BUSIEST AIRPORT Chicago International Airport (O'Hare), which has an aircraft movement every 45 seconds on average.

THE BIRTH OF RAILWAYS

The first regular passenger service was that of the Liverpool and Manchester Railway on 15 September, 1830. The opening of the line caused a sensation. When William Huskisson, an ex-government minister, stepped across the rails to patch up a quarrel with the Duke of Wellington, one of George Stephenson's new locomotives knocked him down. The dying politician was carried off in a train at 58 km/h. Shortly before this the British House of Lords had thought Stephenson crazy for claiming that a speed of 20 km/h would be possible. Many lords thought such a speed would make people's noses bleed. But between 1843 and 1847 a 'railway mania' hit Britain and a huge network developed.

WHEN EAST MET WEST

The building of the American trans-continental railway began from both the east and the west coast in 1865. The Union Pacific Company built west from Omaha and the Central Pacific drove east from Sacramento.

After many mishaps, the joining of the rails took place on 10 May 1869. Top executives of both railroad companies performed a ceremonial driving in of the final spike made of gold but removed after the ceremony.

UNDERGROUND RAILWAYS

The underground railway or 'subway' first ran in London in 1863, when a steam-train operated between Paddington and Farringdon Street. The first electric 'tube' ran from the City to Stockwell in 1890. Undergrounds are either 'cut-and-cover' (basically a trench roofed over) or 'tube' (bored through the earth).

The first 13-km section of the Paris Metro opened on 19 July 1900.

New York's subway – started in 1900 – has 458 stations, more than any other underground railway in the world.

The world's grandest underground stations are in Moscow. They are decorated in marble and granite and embellished with mosaics (above).

RAILWAY RECORDS

- **The longest railway** is the USSR's Trans-Siberian Line. It runs from Moscow to Nakhodka, a seaport on the Pacific Coast, a distance of 9,334 km, a journey which takes over eight days with 97 stops.

- **The highest railway** is at La Cima in Peru where the Morococha branch of the Peruvian State Railways runs at 4,818 metres above sea level.

- **The biggest railway station** in the world is Grand Central Station in New York. Some 550 trains use the 123 tracks and 43 platforms of this station every day.

FIRSTS AT SEA

- FIRST STEAMBOAT PASSENGER SHIP was Robert Fulton's *Clermont*, which operated in the United States from 1807.
- FIRST KNOWN IRON SHIP was a sailing vessel – the British *Vulcan* built in 1818. First known iron steamship was the British *Aaron Manby*, in service in 1821. Steel ships came about 60 years later.
- FIRST STEAMER ACROSS THE ATLANTIC using mainly steam power – but some sail – was the British *Sirius* in 1838.
- FIRST PROPELLER-DRIVEN SHIP was the *Robert F. Stockton*. Its screw propeller was developed by John Ericsson, a Swede in England, and put to commercial use by him in the United States in 1839.
- FIRST NUCLEAR-POWERED submarine, *Nautilus*, was launched by the United States in 1954.
- THE LONGEST PASSENGER LINER ever built is the *France* – 315.5 metres. It was launched in 1962.
- FIRST HOVERCRAFT SERVICE, in Britain, 1962.

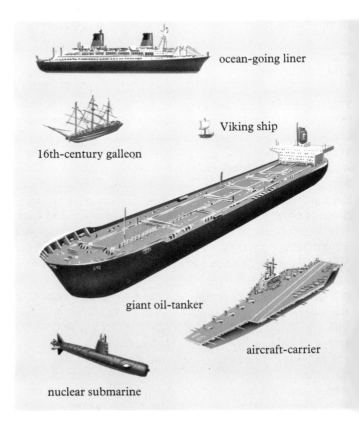

ocean-going liner

16th-century galleon

Viking ship

giant oil-tanker

aircraft-carrier

nuclear submarine

GOMUKU is a pencil and paper game for two. First draw a grid of one hundred squares (right).

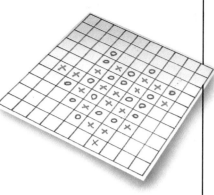

The first player draws a circle in any one of the squares. The other player draws a cross in any square. You take it in turns to draw in the squares, the object being to get five of your symbols in a row. At the same time your opponent is doing the same but you are both also trying to prevent the other player from winning.

When a player gets a row of five symbols draw a line through them and score one point. The person with the most points when the grid is filled wins.

YES AND NO One person asks questions and the other player has to answer as quickly as possible without saying either 'yes' or 'no'. It is amazing how difficult it can be to avoid those two little words!

WORD CHAINS The first player calls out the name of a country (or fruit, bird, etc), then the next player names a country that starts with the last letter of the first country named.

You then continue to take it in turns. If a player cannot name a country with the appropriate letter he or she is out of the game. Here is an example: France, England, Denmark, Korea.

HOW MANY WORDS? Each player has a sheet of paper and a pencil. Given five minutes they write down as many things they can think of beginning and ending with the same letter.

Each player is awarded one point for each word and two points for any word that no-one else has.

WHO AM I? One player thinks of the name of a famous person. The other players ask questions, such as 'Are you a woman?', 'Are you alive?', 'Are you a scientist?', of the first player to try to discover the famous name. Only questions that can be answered with a 'yes' or 'no' are allowed.

When someone guesses who the person is, he or she starts the next round.

KEEPING IN TOUCH

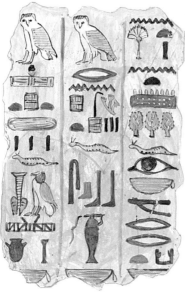

Egyptian hieroglyphic writing.

- WRITTEN COMMUNICATION in picture form (*hieroglyphics*) developed first in Ancient Egypt about 5000 years ago. Modern Chinese characters are simplified picture symbols.

- ALPHABET as it is now known was developed by the Phoenicians over 3000 years ago. They probably adapted a Semitic system derived from Egypt.

- CHEAP BOOKS became possible when printing, invented in China and Korea, was improved technically in Germany in the 1400s. Reading and writing depended upon education. Most people could neither read nor write until the 1800s.

- HUMAN SPEECH became possible only when people developed a pharynx long enough to be able to make speech sounds.

A WORLD LANGUAGE?

In 1887 Lazarus Ludovic Zamenhof (1859–1917) unveiled ESPERANTO, a language he hoped would become universal. Esperanto is now spoken by about eight million people around the world.

Spelling in Esperanto is easy, each letter represents only one sound, and each sound has only one letter. Grammar has been cut down to just sixteen rules.

Zamenhof published his language under the pen name of Dr Esperanto ('one who is hoping').

In the Middle Ages in Europe, people who could not read learned stories from the Bible from pictures in stained-glass windows.

ELECTRICAL COMMUNICATION

TELEGRAPH Samuel Morse sent signals along 518 metres of wire in 1837. In 1845 his work resulted in the opening of the first public telegraph service, from Washington DC to Baltimore.

TELEPHONE was invented by Alexander Graham Bell in the USA in 1876.

GRAMOPHONE (PHONOGRAPH) was invented in the USA by Thomas Edison in 1877.

CINEMATOGRAPHY was developed by Edison between 1890 and 1893.

WIRELESS TELEGRAPHY was invented in 1895 by Guglielmo Marconi, an Italian.

TELEVISION was the result of the work of many scientists. John Logie Baird demonstrated it publicly in January 1926. Vladimir Zworykin (then Russian, later American) applied for a patent in December 1923, and a short-range transmission was made by C. Francis Jenkins in the United States in June 1925. First high definition (405 lines) television was transmitted from London in 1936. Colour came in 1953.

PHOTOCOPYING was invented in 1938.

RADAR, developed by Robert Watson-Watt, could detect aircraft at over 27 kilometres by 1935 and at 161 kilometres by 1938.

SATELLITE *Telstar* relayed television pictures across the Atlantic from 1962.

THE FIRST PRINTED BOOK

The first book to be printed mechanically using moveable type was the Bible in about 1454. It was printed in Mainz, Germany by Johann Gutenberg, and the book is usually referred to as the Gutenberg Bible.

The first English printer was William Caxton who set up a press at Westminster, London, in 1476. Today complete pages are produced by computers, transferred to paper by lasers and photographed onto a printing plate.

A woodcut of Gutenberg

THE FIRST TYPEWRITER

The first modern typewriter was the Sholes and Glidden machine which appeared on the market in 1874. It was designed by Christopher Latham Sholes, together with Samuel W. Soulé and Carlos Glidden. One thousand of the machines were produced by the Remington company.

The first author to produce a typewritten manuscript for a publisher was Mark Twain with his book *Life on the Mississippi*. He used a Sholes and Glidden.

Left: Hammond's typewriter of 1880. A hammer hit the back of the paper pressing it against a letter on a fixed cylinder. The disadvantage was you could not see what you had written without raising the cylinder.

1. Portable *camera obscura*, 1694. An image of the landscape was projected on to paper ready for tracing.

2. Silhouette, 1790. The profile was traced from the shadow cast by a lamp on to a piece of paper.

3. Photography by Niépce, 1827. A photo-sensitive pewter plate replaces the paper of the *camera obscura*.

4. The first Daguerreo-type camera, 1839. Daguerre's process required a much shorter exposure time.

◀ Fox Talbot's picture of Lacock Abbey was made in 1843 using the Calotype process which he had invented in 1841. It was the first negative/positive process and meant that an infinite number of prints could be taken from one negative.

A MATTER OF TOUCH

A blind musician, Louis Braille, was alone in a restaurant in 1834 when he hit upon the idea that was to revolutionize the world of blind people.

Prior to that time blind people had to read from pages of raised letters. Braille's system is much easier to use. It consists of a block of six dots – three dots by two dots – each letter of the alphabet being a different number and combination of dots.

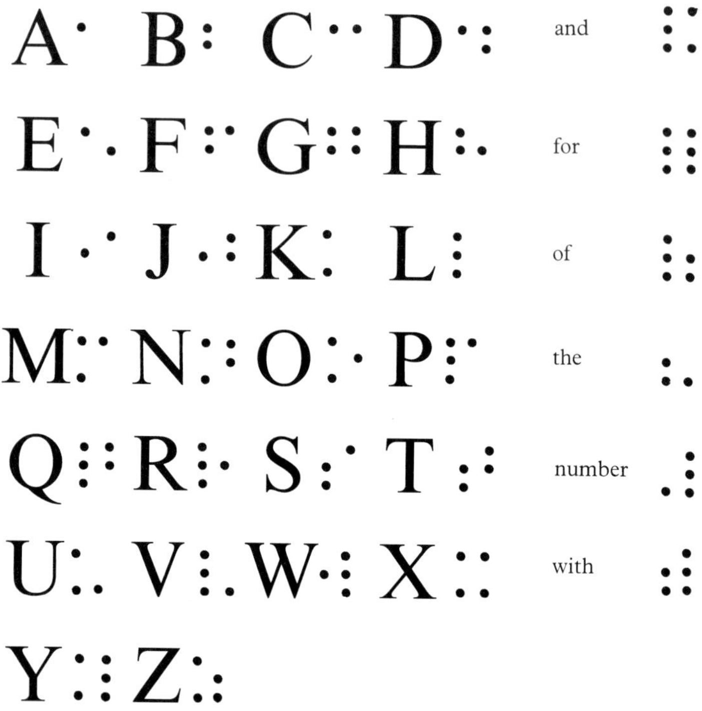

A· B: C·· D··   and   ::

E·. F·· G:: H:.   for   ::

I · J·: K: L: of   :.

M:: N:: O:· P::   the   :.

Q:: R:· S:· T::   number   .:

U:. V:. W·· X::   with   .:

Y:: Z::

BACK TO FRONT

One of the easiest ways to write a secret message is to write all the words back to front. So, instead of writing ELEPHANT you would write TNAHPELE.

Here is a message written like this. Can you work out what it says?

TEEM EM NI EHT TNARUATSER TA YADDIM

SCRAMBLED LETTERS

For this code you must first write down the alphabet. Write down the letters again, under the first set, but in a random order:

A	B	C	D	E	F	G	H	I	J	K	L	M
I	U	V	W	B	R	L	Z	P	H	Q	X	A

N	O	P	Q	R	S	T	U	V	W	X	Y	Z
G	T	F	K	M	Y	E	C	J	S	N	D	O

Both you and the person you are communicating with must have a copy of this code. When you write to your friend in secret you substitute the correct letters of the alphabet for the one in the second line. So, the word MOVED, for example, would be written ATJBW.
Try to decipher this message.

DTCM ZTCYB PY UBPGL SIEVZBW UD YBVMBE ILBGEY

THE MORSE CODE

The Morse Code is a series of dots and dashes that can be transmitted with a flashing light or by telegraph. It was invented by Samuel Morse. The first official message, transmitted by Morse between Baltimore and Washington, USA on 4 May 1844 was 'What hath God wrought?'.

A simple device to send morse-code messages by light flashes.

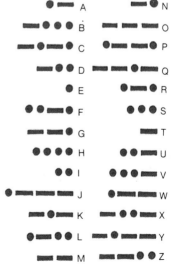

● ▬ A
▬ ● ● ● B
▬ ● ▬ ● C
▬ ● ● D
● E
● ● ▬ ● F
▬ ▬ ● G
● ● ● ● H
● ● I
● ▬ ▬ ▬ J
▬ ● ▬ K
● ▬ ● ● L
▬ ▬ M
▬ ● N
▬ ▬ ▬ O
● ▬ ▬ ● P
▬ ▬ ● ▬ Q
● ▬ ● R
● ● ● S
▬ T
● ● ▬ U
● ● ● ▬ V
● ▬ ▬ W
▬ ● ● ▬ X
▬ ● ▬ ▬ Y
▬ ▬ ● ● Z

SIGNALLING TO AIRCRAFT

If you are stranded in some remote area you should make a large SOS on the ground to show air searchers where you are. Use stones, material or large sticks.

If the searching aircraft can see you, there are hand and body signals which you can use – the semaphore flag code (below) for instance.

The semaphore code was devised in 1767 by a certain Mr Edgenorth to send race results to him from the course while he lay ill in bed!

There are also colour and patterned alphabetical flags. A plain yellow flag, for instance, represents Q; it also means a ship is in quarantine.

A & 1   B & 2   C & 3   D & 4   E & 5   F & 6   G & 7

H & 8   I & 9   J   K & 0   L   M   N

O   P   Q   R   S   T   U

V   W   X   Y   Z   Numeral

SIGN LANGUAGE

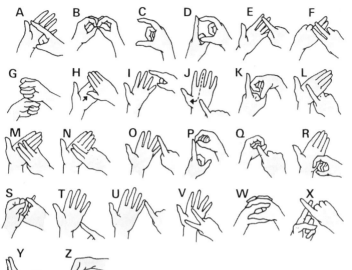

LEADING LINGUIST Cardinal Giuseppe Mezzofanti, (d.1849) could speak 60 languages and could read 114.

Most deaf and dumb people communicate with sign language. The first person to teach sign language was a Spaniard, Pedro Ponce de Lion, in the 16th century.

THE NATO ALPHABET

When communicating over a telephone or radio transmitter it is easy to mishear letters. This problem can be overcome by following each letter with a word beginning with that letter. This is the code used in English-speaking countries:

A Alpha	J Juliet	S Sierra
B Bravo	K Kilo	T Tango
C Charlie	L Lima	U Uniform
D Delta	M Mike	V Victor
E Echo	N November	W Whisky
F Foxtrot	O Oscar	X X-ray
G Golf	P Papa	Y Yankee
H Hotel	Q Quebec	Z Zulu
I India	R Romeo	

HISTORY AND CUSTOMS

HIGHLIGHTS OF HISTORY

c.2600 BC
Pyramids built in
Egypt.
460 BC Age of
Pericles begins in
Athens.
45 BC Julius
Caesar becomes
virtual dictator of
Rome.
4 BC Probable
birth of Jesus at
Bethlehem.

AD

476 End of the
Western Roman
Empire.
570 Mahomet
born in Mecca.
800 Charlemagne
crowned Holy
Roman Emperor.
1000 Leif
Ericsson discovers
Vinland in North
America.
1066 Norman
conquest of
England.
1096 Start of First
Crusade.
1260 Kublai Khan
becomes ruler of
China.

An Etruscan carving.

1291 End of the
Crusades.
1337 Hundred
Year's War
between France
and England
begins.
1341–1351
Bubonic plague
(Black Death)
ravages Europe;
one in four dies.
1431 Joan of Arc
burnt at the stake.
1453 Turks
capture
Constantinople –
end of eastern
Roman Empire.
1492 Christopher
Columbus lands
in the New

World. Muslims
expelled from
Spain.
1517 Martin
Luther nails his
95 theses to door
of Wittenberg
Castle church.
Reformation
begins.
1558 Elizabeth I
becomes Queen of
England.
1564 Birth of
William
Shakespeare.

A crusader knight.

1588 English fleet defeats Spanish Armada.
1607 First English colony in North America founded at Jamestown, Virginia.
1618 Thirty Years' War begins.
1620 *Mayflower* sails to America with Pilgrim Fathers.
1642–6 English Civil War.
1643 Louis XIV becomes King of France.
1696 Peter the Great becomes Tsar of Russia.
1740 Accession of Frederick II (the Great) to throne of Prussia.
1775 American War of Independence (Revolutionary War) begins.
1783 Treaty of Paris ends American War of Independence.
1789 French Revolution.
1799 Napoleon rules France.
1805 Nelson wins Battle of Trafalgar.
1815 Napoleon finally defeated.
1837 Victoria becomes Queen.
1854 Crimean War begins.
1861 American Civil War begins.
1870 Franco-Prussian War begins.
1880 First Boer War.
1898 Spanish-American War.
1904 Russo-Japanese War begins.
1914 Outbreak of First World War.
1917 Russian Revolution.
1933 Adolf Hitler,

A Shakespearean theatre.

Chancellor of Germany.
1936 Civil War begins in Spain.
1939 Second World War begins.
1945 Atomic bombs dropped on Hiroshima and Nagasaki; end of Second World War.
1947 India becomes independent.
1949 Mao Tse-tung establishes Communist regime in China.
1969 First person lands on the Moon.

1979 Islamic republic declared in Iran.
1985 Mikhail Gorbachev, Soviet leader.
1986 Aid programme to combat famine in Ethiopia.
1988 Earthquake in Armenia devastates three cities.
1989–90 Uprisings for more democracy in China suppressed. Uprisings in Eastern Europe succeed. Berlin Wall dismantled.
1990 Iraq's invasion of Kuwait leads to international crisis.

The Apollo 2 rocket.

DISCOVERY AND EXPLORATION

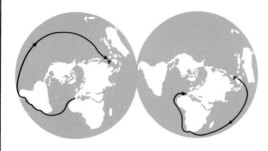

The route taken by Magellan's expedition. 1519–1522 – the first circumnavigation of the world.

- Ferdinand Magellan's ships took three years to circumnavigate the globe. Magellan himself did not complete the journey for he was killed by inhabitants of the Phillipines.

- The coast of North America was known to Viking sailors but it is Christopher Columbus who landed in Cuba in 1492, and reached the American mainland in 1498, to whom the credit goes for discovering the continent.

  Captain Cook explored and charted the coasts of Australia, New Zealand and New Guinea.

- Captain James Cook (1728–1779) made three spectacular voyages around the world which revolutionized knowledge of the southern hemisphere. He claimed Australia for Britain.

- Until the 19th century the centre of Africa was an area of mystery to the rest of the world. This changed following the courageous pioneering explorations of men like James Bruce, David Livingstone, Mungo Park, René Caille, and Henry Morton Stanley who discovered many of the continent's secrets.

THE GREAT VOYAGES

1000 Leif Ericsson (Viking) reaches Newfoundland

1271 Start of the travels of Marco Polo (Venetian)

1487–88 Bartholomew Diaz (Portuguese) rounds Cape of Good Hope

1492–6 Christopher Columbus (Italian) discovers West Indies

1496–1503 Amerigo Vespucci (Florentine) explores Mexico

1497 John Cabot (Genoese) discovers Newfoundland and Nova Scotia

1498 Vasco da Gama (Portuguese) discovers sea route from Europe to India

1500 Pedro Cabral claims Brazil for Portugal

1509 Sebastian Cabot explores American and Brazilian coasts

1519 Ferdinand Magellan (Portuguese) begins first voyage around the world

1520 Cortés (Spanish) conquers Mexico

1534 Jacques Cartier (French) founds La Nouvelle France, the future Canada

1557–80 Francis Drake (English) sails around the world

1606 William Janszoon (Dutch) discovers Australia

1642–44 Abel Tasman (Dutch) discovers New Zealand and Tasmania

1700 William Dampier (British) explores west coast of Australia

1728 Vitus Bering (Danish) discovers Bering Strait

1768–71 Coast of New Zealand and eastern Australia charted by James Cook (British)

1795–97 Mungo Park explores River Niger

1849–73 David Livingstone (Scottish) crosses Africa

1909 Robert Peary (American), first to reach North Pole

1911 Roald Amundsen (Norwegian), reaches South Pole

1929 Admiral R. Byrd (American) first to fly over South Pole

1953 Conquest of Mount Everest by Edmund Hillary (New Zealand) and Sherpa Norgay Tensing (Nepalese)

1958 Nuclear submarine *Nautilus* (American) makes first undersea crossing of the Arctic

1961 Yuri Gagarin (Russian) makes first space flight

1969 Neil Armstrong (American) becomes first person on the Moon

Portuguese caravel of the 1400s.

SPACE EXPLORATION

Sputnik 1 was the world's first artificial satellite. It was 57 cm in diameter, weighed 83 kg and was put into orbit by USSR on 4 October 1957.

● The first living creature to go into space was the dog 'Laika' on 3 November 1957. She made 1,000 orbits in *Sputnik 2.*

● Yuri Alekseyevich Gagarin (1934–68) was the first man in space. In *Vostok 1,* launched on 12 April 1961. he made one orbit of the Earth.

● The first woman in space was the Soviet cosmonaut Valentina Tereshkova on 16 June, 1963 in *Vostok 6.*

● Neil Armstrong became the first person on the Moon on 21 July 1969 when he stepped onto the lunar surface from the steps of the lunar module *Eagle.*

1. Sputnik
2. Laika, the space dog.
3. Yuri Gagarin, the first man in space.
4. Valentina Tereshkova, the first woman in space.
5. Neil Armstrong, the first man on the Moon.
6. The LEVA (Lunar Extra-Vehicular Activity) suit worn by Apollo astronauts.
7. The LRV (Lunar Roving Vehicle) used by American astronauts to travel on the Moon's surface. Built mainly of aluminium and weighing about 181 kilograms, the LRV was 310 cm long, 206 cm wide and 114 cm high.

The word 'satellite' was first used by the astronomer Johannes Kepler in a letter to Galileo Galilei in 1610. The word comes from the Greek word 'satellos' meaning 'attendant'.

● To get into Earth orbit a rocket has to travel at 8 km per second. To escape Earth's gravity completely the rocket will have to travel at 11.5 km per second.

CUSTOMS AROUND THE WORLD

● At EASTER in Greece it is the custom to have someone hold one egg in the palm of their hand while someone bangs another egg against it. The winner is the egg that does not crack with the blow.

● MAY DAY – 1st May – is a day for celebration in many countries. In the northern hemisphere it marks the beginning of summer.

The ancient Romans paid tribute to the goddess of flowers in May. In the British Isles country people danced around a maypole. Also in the British Isles, a strange black hobby horse dances through the streets of Padstow in Cornwall.

In 1899 a gathering of revolutionaries celebrated May Day as a time for all workers to unite. This idea caught on and May Day has been celebrated as a workers' holiday in many parts of the world since.

● Each year, on ASCENSION DAY, the wells of several villages in Derbyshire, England are decorated with beautiful pictures made with flowers. The custom dates back to times when water spirits were worshipped in order to ensure a good supply of fresh water.

● THE FIRST CHRISTMAS CARD appeared in England in 1843. It was designed by J. C. Horsley for his friend Sir Henry Cole. It showed a large family enjoying a Christmas celebration.

FATHER CHRISTMAS The tradition of the man with white whiskers and red cloak who brings presents for children at Christmas originates from St Nicholas, the patron saint of children and sailors.

Among Dutch settlers in New Amsterdam (now New York) he assumed the role of a kindly magician. In Dutch St Nicholas is called Sinter Claes and this has gradually been changed into Santa Claus.

ALL HALLOWS' EVE, or HALLOWE'EN, the night of 31 October is when witches are supposed to take to the skies on broomsticks. It is a time when ghosts are said to roam.

In America and some parts of the British Isles children dress up in ghoulish costumes and go from house to house demanding a 'trick or treat'. Usually you give them a treat of sweets, but if you are foolish enough to say 'trick', anything can happen!

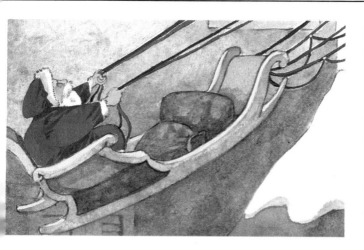

At an annual festival on the island of Cheung Chau, off Hong Kong, over 75,000 towers of bamboo covered with buns are built. The idea is that young men scramble up the towers to collect a bun. The higher they manage to climb the luckier and more prosperous they will be in the years to come.

DECORATING EASTER EGGS

Decorating eggs at Easter is a widespread Christian custom.

To decorate your own eggs, first boil them and, when cool, use felt-tipped pens to draw any design you like on the shell.

Another way is to add some food colouring to the water in which you boil the eggs.

If you want to have patterns on the eggs, boil the eggs as normal, then stick some patterned shapes onto the shell. Return the egg to the pan but add the food colouring to the water. After a while remove the eggs from the water, allow them to cool and then remove the shapes.

To polish eggs, use a little cooking oil and rub with a soft cloth.

HALLOWE'EN LANTERN

Hallowe'en lanterns can be made with pumpkins, turnips or swedes.

Cut off the top and then scoop out all the flesh from the inside of the vegetable. Be careful that you do not go through the sides.

The flesh can be saved for cooking.

With a knife, cut holes in one side to make two eyes, a nose and a mouth.

Use some melted wax to fix a candle to a shallow tin.

Place the candle and tin tray into the lantern. Light the candle (be careful as you do this).

Place the top back on and your hallowe'en lantern is complete.

How to make a Hallowe'en lantern.

AMERICAN THANKSGIVING

On the fourth Thursday in November Americans celebrate '*Thanksgiving*', the anniversary of the day when the Pilgrim Fathers landed in the New World in 1620. On the first Thanksgiving Day turkey formed the main meal and it remains the traditional Thanksgiving dish to this day. Other foods found on American tables on this important festival include pumpkin pie and baked ham with a delicious raisin sauce.

PAPIER-MÂCHÉ

Half-fill a washing-up bowl with wallpaper paste and cut up small strips of newspaper. Smear the object that you want to make a model from with vaseline. Dip the strips of newspaper, one at a time, into the paste and lay the strips over the model base until it is covered with several layers of paper. Leave to dry and remove model.

PAPER LANTERNS

Take a sheet of coloured paper, measuring about 20 cm by 25 cm.

Fold the paper in half and cut slits in it, from the fold almost to the opposite edges. Open out the paper and glue the ends together.

Take another sheet of paper, the same size but a different colour from the first. Roll it into a tube and then push it into the middle of the lantern.

A small strip of paper attached to the top will make a handle so you can hang the lanterns up for any festive occasion.

THE WORLD OF ART

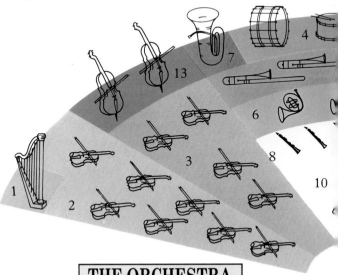

THE ORCHESTRA

The instruments of an orchestra form four principal groups: woodwind, brass, percussion and strings. The numbers of instruments in a typical orchestra is as follows:

STRINGS
First violins (any number)
Second violins (any number)
Violas (any number)
Cellos (any number)
Double basses (any number)

WOODWIND
Flutes   (2)
Oboes   (2)
Clarinets   (2)
Bassoons   (2)

BRASS
Horns   (4)
Trumpets   (2)
Trombones   (3)
Tuba   (1)

PERCUSSION
Timpani   (up to 3)
Other percussion instruments as required (these can include tambourines, triangles, cymbals and side drums).

Orchestral Arrangement:
Instruments in an orchestra are usually positioned in the same arrangement:

1. Harp
2. First violins
3. Second violins
4. Timpani and drums
5. Percussion
6. Horns
7. Trumpets, trombones, and tuba
8. Clarinets
9. Bassoons
10. Flutes
11. Oboes and cors anglais
12. Violas
13. Double basses
14. Cellos

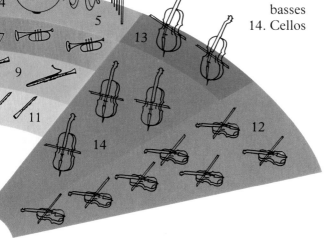

HOW TO CONDUCT

These diagrams show the strokes made by a conductor (from the conductor's point of view) when beating time with a baton.

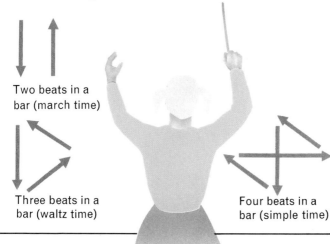

Two beats in a bar (march time)

Three beats in a bar (waltz time)

Four beats in a bar (simple time)

MAKE YOUR OWN MUSIC

If you and your friends make some of the musical instruments described here, you can form your own orchestra.

Anything that produces a noise can be used. Experiment with different things to see what sounds they produce.

When you and your fellow musicians have rehearsed you could use a tape recorder to record your music.

MARACCAS You will need two empty plastic bottles, some small pebbles and some modelling clay.

Put some pebbles in each bottle and then seal the neck of the bottle with the modelling clay.

Shaking the bottles in time to the music produces a good sound for the percussion section of your orchestra.

Experiment with different containers, such as cans, and different things inside them – sand, dried beans, buttons or beads, for example.

BOTTLE XYLOPHONE
This uses bottles containing varying amounts of water.

Use eight bottles and use a musical instrument, such as a piano, to check that you have the correct amount of water in each to produce the eight notes of an octave.

By tapping the bottles with a stick in each hand you will be able to play tunes.

Glue some sandpaper to two blocks of wood. If you rub them together in time with the music you can produce quite a pleasant sound. Try different types of sandpaper.

BAND BANJO You will need a flat tin or cardboard box, six elastic bands, and six sticks each 2 cm long.

Place the elastic bands around the tin. Put each stick under each of the bands.

If you pluck a band with your finger it will make a sound. If you move the stick to a different position you will get a different note. Put all six sticks in different positions and you have six different notes.

BALLET TERMS

arabesque Position in which dancer stands on one leg with arms extended, body bent forward from hips, while other leg is stretched out backwards.

attitude Position in which dancer stretches one leg backwards, bending it a little at the knee so that the lower part of leg is parallel to floor.

ballerina Female ballet dancer.

barre Exercise bar fixed to classroom wall at hip level; dancers grasp it when exercising.

battement Beating movement made by raising and lowering leg, sideways, backwards, or forwards.

choreography Art of dance composition.

classical or traditional ballet includes such works as *Sleeping Beauty*, *Nutcracker* and *Swan Lake*, all created by the Russian composer Tchaikovsky. Among other classical ballets are *Giselle*, *Coppelia* and *La Sylphide*.

corps de ballet Main body of ballet dancers, as distinct from soloists.

entrechat Leap in which dancer rapidly crosses and uncrosses feet in air.

fouetté Turn in which dancer whips free leg round.

glissade Gliding movement.

jeté Leap from one foot to another.

pas Any dance step.

pas de deux Dance for two.

pas seule Solo dance.

pirouette Movement in which dancer spins completely round on one foot.

pointes Tips of dancer's toes, on which many movements are executed.

port de bras Arm movements.

positions Five positions of feet on which ballet is based. These were devised by the French King Louis the Fourteenth's dancing master, Pierre Beauchamp. (see page 118).

BALLET

THE FIVE POSITIONS
There are five positions of
the arms and feet in ballet.
You can use them in many
different ways, such as the
first position of the feet and
fourth position of the arms.
Every ballet step and
movement begins and ends
in one of these positions.

First position

Second position

Third position

Fourth position

Fifth position

THE SEVEN MOVEMENTS
All the movements used in
ballet are based on seven
natural movements. These
are bending, stretching,
rising, sliding, turning,
darting and jumping. Try
each one yourself.

Plier means 'to bend'.

This arabesque penchée
uses a bending movement.

Glissade means 'slide'.

A pirouette is a turning
step.

A pas-de-chat uses darting
and jumping.

The human body can be
divided up into sections to
keep proportions right.

Straight lines appear to
converge at one place,
called the vanishing point.

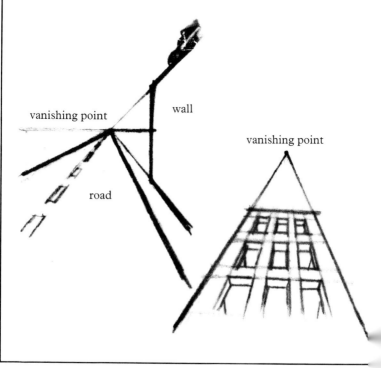

vanishing point

wall

road

vanishing point

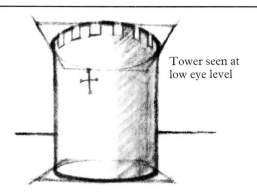

Tower seen at low eye level

A circle in a square will appear as an ellipse when the drawing is tilted away from the eye.

The top of the tower is a circle, and will look like an ellipse at various eye-levels.

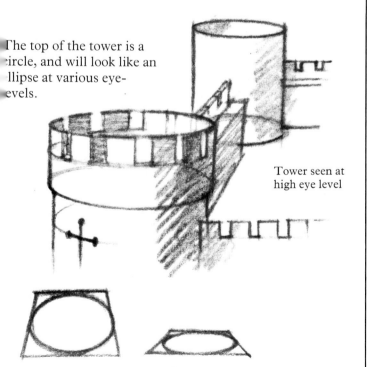

Tower seen at high eye level

High eye level   Low eye level

GREAT ARCHITECTURE

The LEANING TOWER OF PISA was built in 1174. Unfortunately the land on which it was built is a mixture of river mud and sand and the tower began to sink in the ground. The builders tried to correct the tilt by varying the length of the pillars on each storey to add weight on the side opposite the tilt, but to no avail. In 1990 the Tower was closed to tourists.

SIR CHRISTOPHER WREN (1632–1723) is regarded as England's greatest architect. But he had no training in architecture. He was a Professor of Astronomy at Oxford University!

When the great Gothic cathedral that stood on the site of the present St Paul's was destroyed by the Great Fire of London in 1666, King Charles II appointed Wren a Commissioner for rebuilding the City of London. Wren wanted the new St Paul's to be the central point of the rebuilt city but these plans were never realized.

When Wren died at the age of 91, he was buried in the great cathedral he had created. Inscribed on a stone tablet are the words 'Si monumentum requiris, circumspice' ('If you seek his monument, look around you').

THE TAJ MAHAL, near Agra in India took 20,000 workmen 20 years to build. It was built by the Mughal emperor Shah Jehan (1614–1666) as a tomb for his favourite wife, Mumtaz Mahal.

It is built of white marble inlaid with precious stones.

The Great Model of St Paul's Cathedral, made in 1673.

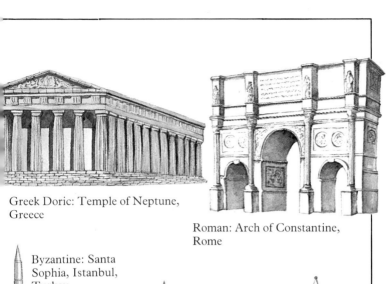

Greek Doric: Temple of Neptune, Greece

Roman: Arch of Constantine, Rome

Byzantine: Santa Sophia, Istanbul, Turkey

Renaissance: Florence Cathedral, Italy

Modern: Empire State Building, New York (1920s)

Gothic: Bourges Cathedral, France

Sydney Opera House, Australia (1960s)

SPORT AND HOBBIES

SPORT: AMERICAN FOOTBALL

The field of play used for American football is known as the GRIDIRON because it is divided by markings at intervals along the whole length of the pitch. The game is derived from rugby and was developed as a college sport towards the end of the 19th century.

As in Rugby, American football uses an oval ball.

The game consists mostly of tackling, passing and running, with very little kicking. The game is played by two teams of 11 men. The yardlines cross the field (120 yards long × $53\frac{1}{3}$ yards wide) every 5 yards. Two rows of *hashmarks* parallel the sidelines in the centre of the field. All play starts with the ball between or on the *hashmarks*. The principal object of the game is to carry the ball over the opponents' goal line. This is a *touchdown* worth six points.

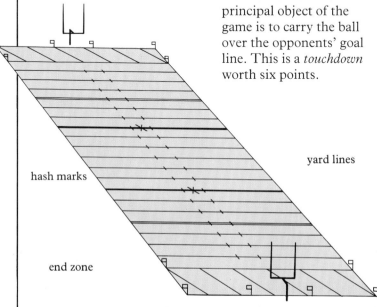

yard lines

hash marks

end zone

RUGBY UNION

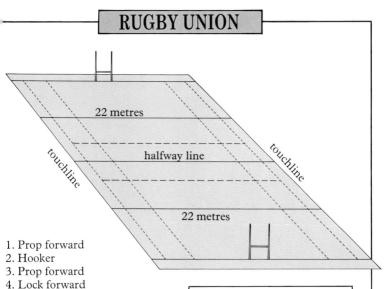

1. Prop forward
2. Hooker
3. Prop forward
4. Lock forward
5. Lock forward
6. Left flank forward
7. Right flank forward
8. Forward
9. Scrum half
10. Outside half
11. Left wing threequarter
12. Left centre threequarter
13. Right centre threequarter
14. Right wing threequarter
15. Full back

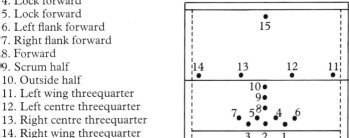

During a game of football at Rugby School, England, in 1823 a 16-year-old schoolboy, William Webb Ellis, picked up the ball and ran with it. While catching the ball was quite usual in the various forms of football played at that time running with the ball was not. The idea caught on and by 1841 the practice was an accepted part of the game at Rugby. The game became popular in other parts of England and nowadays it is played in many countries all over the world.

Duration of game 80 min (2 × 40)
No. per side 15 (2 substitutes, for injury only)
Scoring *try* 4 points, *conversion* 2, *penalty goal* 3, *dropped goal* 3
Ruling body International Rugby Football Board
Major competitions Five Nations Championship (England, France, Ireland, Scotland, Wales), Ranfurly Shield (New Zealand)
Touring sides British Lions (GB), All Blacks (New Zealand), Wallabies (Australia), Tricolors (France)

ASSOCIATION FOOTBALL

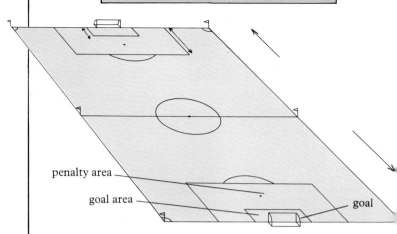

penalty area

goal area

goal

The World Cup is held every four years, and has been won by Brazil (3 times), Italy (3), West Germany (2), Uruguay (2), Argentina (2) and England.

In Britain the most important tournaments, the Football Association Challenge Cup (first played in 1872) and the Football League (formed 1888), with their Scottish counterparts, are the oldest competitions in the world. Since 1956 competitions have been organized between European clubs, principally the European Champions' Cup. The main winners have been Real Madrid (6), Liverpool (3), Bayern Munich (3), Ajax Amsterdam (3), Inter Milan (2), AC Milan (2), Benfica (2), and Nottingham Forest (2).

Outside Europe, South America contains the strongest teams.

Soccer is played all over the world. It is played with a round ball on a rectangular pitch which can be from 90 to 118 metres long. Each team of 11 players score by kicking the ball into the opponents' goal. One of the players is the goalkeeper who is allowed to handle the ball within the goal area. Other players can play the ball with any part of their body except the hands. A game lasts for 90 minutes (two halves of 45 minutes). The governing body is the Fédération Internationale de Football Association.

The FIFA World Cup, played for every four years, is the leading tournament for national soccer teams.

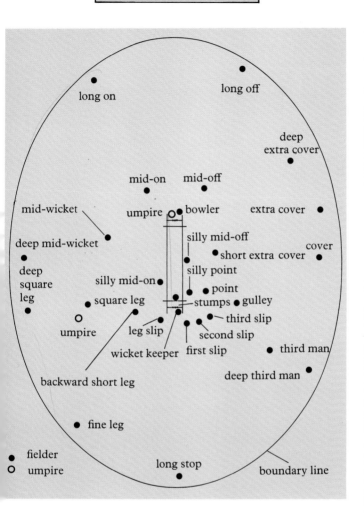

Cricket was probably first played in the 1300s in England. The early bats were curved, and there were no wickets. But by the early 1800s the game was very much as it is now. The pitch is 22 yards (20 metres) from wicket to wicket; the three stumps are 28 inches (71.1 cm) high and 9 inches (22.9 cm) wide. The ball must weigh between $5\frac{1}{2}$ and $5\frac{3}{4}$ ounces (156 and 163 grams); the bat must not be more than $4\frac{1}{4}$ inches (10.8 cm) wide.

The Marylebone Cricket Club (M.C.C.), whose ground is at Lords in London, was started in 1787. It governed the game for many years. The governing body is now the International Cricket Conference.

TENNIS

Lawn tennis as we know it today began in 1874 when a Major Wingfield devised a portable court for playing the ancient game of real tennis. In the following year the tennis committee of the Marylebone Cricket Club issued a code of laws. Other changes followed and in 1888 a Lawn Tennis Association was formed to administer the game.

The game called real

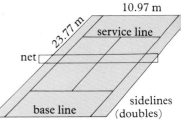

tennis was played in a walled court. The oldest existing court is at Hampton Court Palace, near London, which was built for Henry VIII in 1530.

THE OLYMPICS

The earliest record of the OLYMPIC GAMES was at Olympia on the west coast of Greece in 776 BC. They continued to be held every four years until AD 394 when they were stopped by the Emperor Theodosius.

The modern Olympics were the brainchild of a French baron, Pierre de Coubertin. The first international Olympic Games were opened in Athens by the King of Greece on 6 April, 1896. Since then they have been held every four years with the exceptions of 1916, 1940 and 1944 when two World Wars intervened.

● The SYMBOL used at the Olympic Games shows five linked circles. The circles represent the continents of Africa, America, Asia, Australasia and Europe.

● The official MOTTO of the Olympic Games is Citius, Altius, Fortius which in Latin means Swifter, Higher, Stronger.

BASEBALL

It is said that the game of BASEBALL – America's national sport – was invented by Abner Doubleday in 1839. He is said to have laid out the first diamond (the name given to the pitch) at Copperstown in New York State. Doubleday went on to become a hero in the American Civil War.

Always ask for permission to camp on private land.

Pitch your tent away from trees if possible – to avoid the risk of falling branches. Don't pitch your tent on sloping ground – you may roll out of the tent in the night!

Do not camp too near the water's edge – in case of flooding.

For stays of several days the positioning of the tent, cooking area, and lavatory area is particularly important. Look at the trees to get an indication of the prevailing winds. Pitch your tent so the wind blows from the tent to the kitchen area and then towards the latrines.

● Before making a camp fire cut out a piece of turf large enough for the fire. Keep the turf watered, in a shady spot. When you pack up camp the fire area should be watered and the turf replaced.

● The same applies to turf cut out for the latrine area, which should be a good distance from the tent itself. For one or two campers the latrine can be a small trench a metre long and 30 cm deep.

● A large sheet of polythene can make a useful tent in an emergency. Guy ropes can be attached by tying the rope around a smooth stone, or a ball of mud.

SWIMMING

If you cannot swim ask at your local swimming pool about lessons as it is best to learn from someone else.

You should first learn how to be at home in the water. Fill a wash basin with water and practise putting your face into it. Now try opening your eyes while your face is under water.

You can also practise at home the technique of breathing used by swimmers. Take a deep breath before putting your face into the basin of water. Blow out your breath, lift your face from the water to take another breath, put your face in the water and breathe out, come out of the water and take another breath. Repeat this often.

You can also practise swimming strokes at home well before trying them out in water. You can do this lying on the floor or across the seat of a chair.

SWIMMING DON'TS

Don't swim from a beach where a red flag is flying. The flag indicates it is dangerous to go bathing.

Don't swim near rocks. They create currents which could prove dangerous.

Don't swim too soon after a meal.

Don't swim from a deserted beach. If you do get into trouble there will be no-one around to help you.

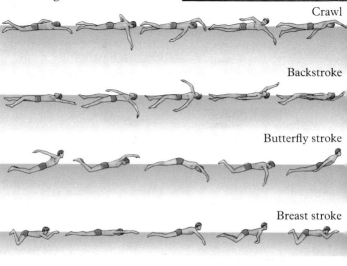

Crawl

Backstroke

Butterfly stroke

Breast stroke

FOSSIL HUNTING

HOW FOSSILS ARE FORMED: 1. Ammonites, the fossil remains of extinct molluscs, are quite common. 2. When the ammonite died, it was buried in the sea bed. 3. The animal dissolved away to form a hollow fossil shell. 4. If the mould was filled with sediment, a cast was formed.

Fossils are the petrified remains of animals or plants, some of which are millions of years old. Limestone, shale, sandstone, coal and chalk areas are the most likely source of fossils. You will not find anything in areas where the rocks are hard. Search in areas where the rock has been exposed recently. Quarries are often a good source of fossils. Quarries are dangerous places: get permission from the site owners and let an adult know where you are going.)

● You will need a hammer and a chisel for breaking the rock, some sheets of paper in which to wrap the fossils, and a bag to carry everything.

● Fossil hunters must have patience for it can take years to build up a good collection. But fossils are fascinating as they will give you an insight into the type of plants and creatures that lived on Earth millions of years ago.

SEARCHING FOR TREASURE

Many archaeologists oppose treasure hunting with metal detectors because of the danger of disturbing archaeological sites. So check with your local library or museum to find out where you can go without causing any damage.

If you find something that may be of importance report it at once, without digging up the whole area. Record your finds. Every six months or so report them to your local museum.

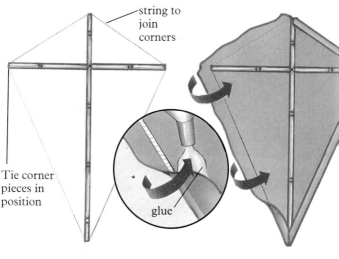

string to
join
corners

Tie corner
pieces in
position

glue

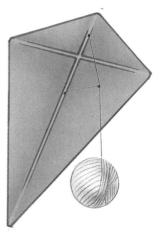

You will need thin
material about
1 metre × 75 cm, thin sticks,
a ball of string, sticky tape,
glue, scissors, thread.

Choose two sticks. One
stick must be twice as long
as the other. Make a cross
shape and bind together
with string. Join the
corners with string or short
sticks to make a diamond
shape.

Lay the frame on top of the
piece of material. Cut the
material around the frame
leaving about 4 cm all
round. Fold over the
material to cover the frame
and sew or glue down the
folds.

Make a tail for your kite
using a piece of string
about twice as long as the
kite. Glue or tie the tail to
the tip of the kite. Attach
two strings to the long stick
of the frame – one below
and one above the cross-
over point. Join the two
ends together and tie them
on to the end of the ball of
string.

MAKE A PERISCOPE

You will need a cardboard box, two small mirrors and adhesive tape. The actual size of your periscope will depend upon the size of mirrors you use.

From the cardboard cut four pieces measuring 8 cm by 30 cm. Tape them together to form a square tube. On one side of the tube, and about 4 cm from the top, cut a small window. Do the same on the opposite side near to the bottom.

Insert one mirror, face-up into the bottom of the tube. Position it so it rests at an angle between the front and rear sides of the tube. Tape into position.

Put the second mirror in a similar position at the top

of the tube. The reflective surface of the two mirrors should face each other. Now cut two squares of card to fit the tube ends.

By looking in through one of the holes you see through the other hole and this enables you to look over walls.

MAKE A HIDE

You can make quite an elaborate hide from four upright sticks over which is draped some fabric covered with twigs and leaves.

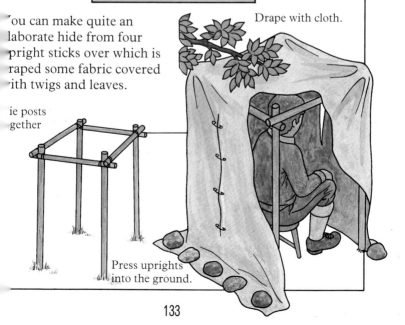

Tie posts together

Drape with cloth.

Press uprights into the ground.

133

There are three main types of fishing – coarse fishing which covers most freshwater fishing except for salmon and trout; fly fishing, in which a fly (usually artificial) is used as a bait to catch trout and salmon; and sea fishing.

It is only by fishing regularly and often that you will become expert at your chosen branch of fishing.

Coarse fishing is carried on in inland waters such as lakes, rivers canals and gravel pits. Most fishing is done with a rod while floats and weights allow the bait to dangle in the water at a chosen depth or to lie on the bottom. The bait can be left in the water, or it can be drawn through it to attact the fish.

The type of fishing and the fish that you will catch depend largely on the area in which you live. Tackle should be chosen with local conditions in mind. Any fishing tackle dealer will be glad to offer advice and help.

RODS The most essential part of an angler's equipment is the rod. Start with an 'all-purpose' rod and add to your tackle collection as and when you are able. The best all round length for a rod is 3.3 metres – made of glass fibre, it need not be expensive.

REELS The traditional fishing reels were centrepin reels and these are still widely used. These reels consist simply of a drum which is on a central spindle. The line is pulled out by the weight of the cast and by the fish, and wound back with a handle. Fixed spool reels are the most popular for all types of fishing where bait or spinners are used. They have a fast recovery rate due to gears built around the handle.

LINES are generally sold on 100-metre spools and are made of nylon. They are graded according to breaking strain.

HOOKS come in different shapes and sizes and success often rests on the hook you choose. It is usually the size of the hook that is most important. They come in various numbered sizes from 1 (the largest) to 20.

NETS Every angler should have two nets. The landing net is used to land a fish that has been played out, so that the angler is able to unhook it. The keep net is a long net with a series of hoops which allow fish to swim freely within it until they are returned to the water at the end of the day.

Most anglers begin by FLOAT FISHING. The baited hook is kept in position by passing the line through a float. When the fish takes the bait the float dips below the water surface.

In LEGERING the bait is presented on the bottom and held there by means of weights (non-lead) through which the line is threaded

WHERE TO FISH You cannot fish anywhere you like. You may well need a licence. This is issued by the local Water Authority. A rod licence only allows you to fish with one rod. You can get your licence at a tackle shop. You will need permission to fish on most waters.

There is a close season for coarse fish to allow them time to spawn and recover before being caught. For most of England and Wales this is from 15th March to 15th June. Scotland and Ireland have no close season.

● The most famous book on angling is *The Compleat Angler* by Isaac Walton, which was published in 1653.

● The best time to catch fish is very early in the morning and during or just after rain. As a general rule the colder the day the better.

SAILING

Sailing requires skill, knowledge and experience. Three basic manoeuvres all sailors must know are:
1. Sailing to windward (into the wind). The boat *tacks* or zigzags at a 45° angle to the direction of the wind.
2. *Reaching*, sailing across the wind or with the wind *abeam*. 3. *Running* or sailing with the wind. The sail is almost at a right angle with the direction of the wind.

When a boat is sailing with the wind blowing over the port side it is said to be on a **port tack**. With the wind coming over the starboard side it would have been on a **starboard tack**.

You must always remember your life-jacket. Most sailing clubs will not allow anyone aboard a dinghy without one.

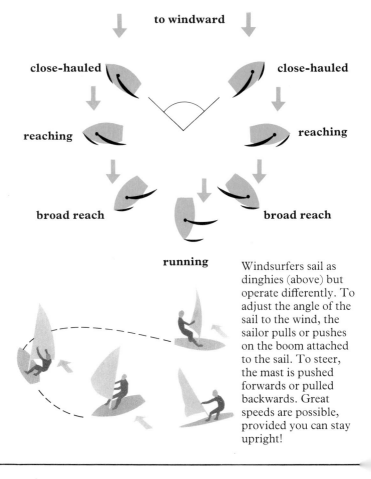

to windward

close-hauled   **close-hauled**

reaching   **reaching**

broad reach   **broad reach**

running

Windsurfers sail as dinghies (above) but operate differently. To adjust the angle of the sail to the wind, the sailor pulls or pushes on the boom attached to the sail. To steer, the mast is pushed forwards or pulled backwards. Great speeds are possible, provided you can stay upright!

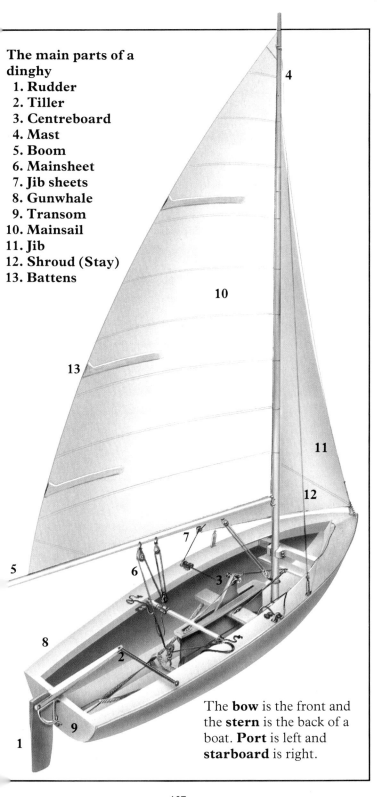

The main parts of a dinghy
1. Rudder
2. Tiller
3. Centreboard
4. Mast
5. Boom
6. Mainsheet
7. Jib sheets
8. Gunwhale
9. Transom
10. Mainsail
11. Jib
12. Shroud (Stay)
13. Battens

The **bow** is the front and the **stern** is the back of a boat. **Port** is left and **starboard** is right.

PICKING THE RIGHT SIZE
Riding a bike that is either too big or too small is dangerous.

First divide your height by three. The answer will give you the ideal frame measurement from the base of the saddle to the pedal crank.

Next measure the distance from your elbow to the fingertips. This distance should be about the same as the distance from the front of the saddle to the rear of the handlebars.

Finally, measure your inside leg. Divide this distance by ten and add the answer to your inside leg measurement. This will give you the ideal distance from the ground to the top of the saddle.

The 'penny farthing' of 1883.

To adjust the saddle loosen the bolt that secures the saddle pillar in the frame (see page 139). Now move the saddle up or down to the height you want. Tighten the bolt and then sit on the saddle to test the height. You should be able to sit on the saddle with both feet touching the ground.

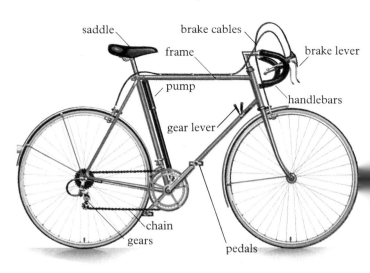

saddle
brake cables
frame
brake lever
pump
handlebars
gear lever
chain
gears
pedals

To adjust the height of the handlebars first loosen the expansion bolt at the top of the handlebars (see above). To do this place a block of wood on top of the bolt and then hit the wood gently with a hammer. This will release a plug at the base of the handlebar stem and you should now be able to loosen the bolt with a spanner.

Stand with your feet on either side of the front wheel and move the handlebars from side to side and either up or down until they are at the height you want. Make sure the handlebars are straight and then re-tighten the expansion bolt.

If, when sitting on the bike, you cannot reach the handlebars comfortably adjust the position of the saddle. Loosen the clamp nut attaching the saddle to the top of its pillar. You can now move the saddle either backwards or forwards.

RULES FOR CYCLISTS

- Always signal correctly and keep your eyes open for other traffic.
- Make sure you know what the traffic signs mean.
- Wear bright clothing so you can be seen night and day.
- When undertaking any maneouvre, make sure your intentions are clear and that you are aware of vehicles and pedestrians nearby.
- Never carry passengers on your bike; never balance anything on the handlebars.
- Make sure you have good lights both front and rear.
- Don't try to ride a bike that is too big for you.
- Always let someone know where you are going when you go out on your bike.
- Regularly check brakes, lights, and tyres.

HOW TO REPAIR A PUNCTURE

Pump air into the tyre. Wet your finger and transfer your saliva to the valve. If a bubble forms the fault is in the valve and it will need replacing.

If the valve is working normally you will have to check the inner tube.

Remove the wheel and take out the valve to release any air still in the tube.

Pinch the tyre all the way around near to the edge of the wheel rim.

Push a tyre lever (1) under the tyre between the tyre and the inner tube. (In an emergency use the handle of a spoon.) Insert another tyre lever about 15 cm from the first.

Force the edge of the tyre over the wheel rim. Do this all the way round.

You can now pull out the inner tube (2).

Replace the valve in the inner tube and pump some air into it (3). If the puncture is large you should be able to see it quickly. If not, put the inner tube into water (4). Do this bit by bit until you see air bubbles coming from the inner tube. The air bubbles show you where the puncture is. Dry the inner tube and mark the puncture with a crayon (5).

Let all the air out of the inner tube and rub around the area of the puncture with sandpaper (6).

Put rubber cement around the area of the puncture (7).

Take a patch from your puncture repair outfit, remove the backing, and place the patch on the cemented area. Hold it in position (8).

Sprinkle powdered chalk over the patch to absorb any excess rubber solution.

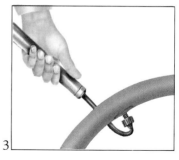

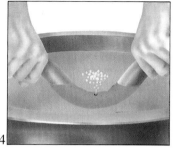

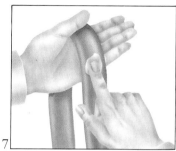

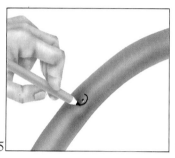

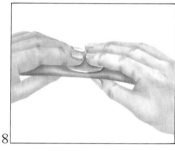

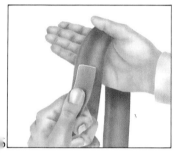

Push the inner tube back into the tyre and make sure that the valve goes through the hole in the wheel rim.

Starting from the valve press the tyre back into the wheel rim. Go all the way round the wheel doing this. Repeat on the other side of the wheel (9).

Tighten the valve nut and pump the tyre up.

You can now go on your way once again.

KEEP IT CLEAN

Reduce the amount of cleaning you do by applying a thin coating of vaseline mixed with petrol to the chromed part of the bicycle. Before the petrol in the mixture has time to evaporate, use an old paintbrush to paint the liquid over the chromed parts. Clean off with a cloth.

RIDING

Today, most people ride purely for pleasure. It takes a great deal of skill to ride a horse well. Some people test their skill by riding in competitions, in jumping, cross-country events and various sports such as polo.

It takes a lot of patience and practice to ride well. One of the most important things a rider must learn is how to tell a horse what to do. There are two kinds of signals used for this. The first, known as natural aids, are given by hand, leg and voice commands. The second are artificial aids. Those include using riding sticks and spurs.

Command signals must be given smoothly and correctly, otherwise the horse will become confused about what the rider wants it to do.

Correct

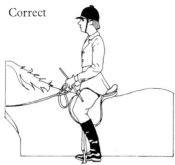

Incorrect

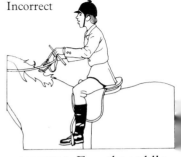

Bottom: The four gaits of a horse, from left : walk, trot, canter, gallop.

MOUNTING: Face the saddle and hold the reins in both hands. Put left foot in the left stirrup, which is held by the right hand. Swing right leg over the horse's back to arrive – lightly – in the saddle (opposite).

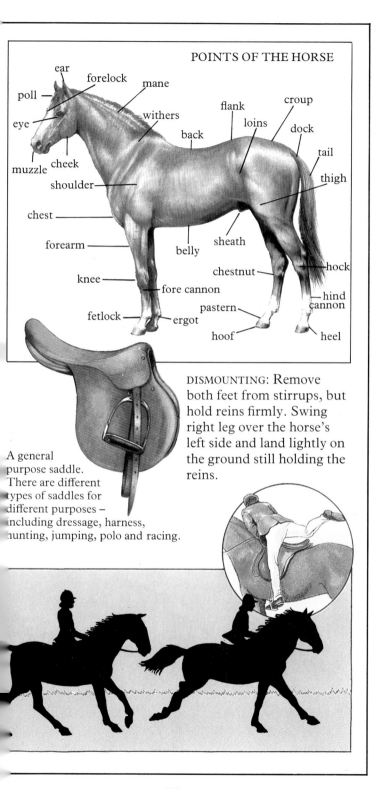

POINTS OF THE HORSE

ear
forelock
mane
poll
eye
withers
muzzle
cheek
shoulder
chest
forearm
knee
fetlock
ergot
fore cannon
belly
flank
loins
croup
dock
back
tail
thigh
sheath
chestnut
hock
hind cannon
pastern
hoof
heel

A general purpose saddle. There are different types of saddles for different purposes – including dressage, harness, hunting, jumping, polo and racing.

DISMOUNTING: Remove both feet from stirrups, but hold reins firmly. Swing right leg over the horse's left side and land lightly on the ground still holding the reins.

Don't stand with the Sun directly behind you. This casts dark shadows and you will probably find that your friends have their eyes shut! Have the Sun on one side of you.

● Hold the camera steady. Try supporting your elbows on a fence or the bonnet of a car.

● Try looking from different viewpoints before taking the photograph.

● When photographing people do not always have them facing the camera. If there is a nice view or an interesting building nearby it is more natural that they should be looking at that.

● The best pictures are taken when the subject is unaware. Such candid shots add life to a picture.

It is important to focus the camera lens properly. The top photograph is only partly in focus.

A PIN-HOLE CAMERA

The pin-hole camera shows the camera principle in its most basic form. Light enters the box through a tiny hole, forming an upside down image on a translucent screen. You can make a pin-hole camera with a cardboard box – a shoe box is ideal.

Make a small hole in the centre of one end. At the opposite end cut a square window and cover it with a tracing paper screen, using sticky tape to hold it in place.

Hold the box with the pin-hole facing the window on a bright day. You should be able to see the scene outside, upside down, on the screen.

CHESS

Chess probably originated in India in the 5th century. It was adapted by the Persians from whom the Arabs got the game. As a result of the Moorish occupation of Spain the game became known in Europe, although it was not until the 15th century that modern chess began to evolve.

● The largest chess game in the world is played at Marostica, Italy. In the piazza is an area of marble squares on which human actors dress up as chess pieces every second year.

The opening positions of the pieces on a chess board.

Pawns

Rook   Bishop   King   Knight
  Knight   Queen   Bishop   Rook

Pawn   Rook   Knight   Bishop   Queen   King

1 The bishop's move is diagonal and can travel until blocked by an occupied square.

2 The knight's move is L-shaped and can be made in any direction.

3 The rook moves in straight lines and can travel until blocked by an occupied square.

4 The queen can move in any direction and can travel until blocked by an occupied square.

5 The king can move in any direction – one square at a time.

6 Except on their first move, pawns move one square at a time.

START A COLLECTION

Collecting things can be an inexpensive hobby. You could, for example, collect postcards from places you visit, the labels from different cheeses, wrappers from chocolate bars, buttons, cartoons from magazines, theatrical posters, sports programmes – anything you fancy. Several people have found that collecting things for fun can turn into a full-time hobby and a few have had their collections end up in museums!

COLLECTING POSTCARDS

Postcards can be bought from places you visit on holiday, bought from second-hand shops, or sent to you by friends.

If you wish you can specialize in old postcards, views of a particular area, or humorous cards. Keep your cards in boxes or albums.

COLLECTING CHEESE LABELS

is popular. You can buy cheese labels from specialist dealers or swap them with other collectors. The cheapest way to start a collection is to persuade the shoppers in the family to buy a different cheese each time they go shopping.

Use stamp hinges to stick your labels in an album.

COLLECTING COINS

Many people have started collecting coins after coming back from holiday abroad with a few foreign coins left over. Some people collect old coins of a particular country because of their historical interest.

The cheapest way to start a coin collection is to concentrate on foreign coins obtained from friends returning from abroad.

CLEANING COINS

To clean copper coins, mix together one part salt to four parts vinegar. Dip your coins in this liquid for a minute and they will come up shining like new.

Do not use this liquid for coins that may be valuable. Get experienced advice.

COLLECTING AUTOGRAPHS

To start with you could just collect the signatures of your family and friends. You can then try to get the autographs of some famous people. The most satisfying way to do this is to meet the people themselves. Failing this you could write to people you admire and ask them for their autograph. You can even buy autographs of famous people from other collectors.

Keep your autographs in an autograph book.

Coins of unusual shape and coins with animals in their design make interesting subjects for a collection.

147

STAMP COLLECTING

Stamp collecting is the most popular hobby in the world. The earliest reference to stamp collecting was in *The Times* in 1841, just one year after the introduction of the postage stamp, when the following advertisement was published:

'A young lady, being desirous of covering her dressing-room with cancelled postage stamps, has been so far encouraged in her wish by private friends as to have succeeded in collecting 16,000. These, however, being insufficient, she will be greatly obliged if any good-natured person who may have these (otherwise useless) little articles at their disposal, would assist her in her whimsical project.'

Modern stamp collectors would be appalled at the 'misuse' of stamps!

Because there are now so many stamps in the world, collectors tend to specialize. They may collect only stamps of a particular country, of a special period, or stamps relating to one particular subject, such as birds, the theatre or sport.

REMOVING STAMPS FROM PAPER

Never try to tear the stamp off the envelope or package.

1 First cut around the stamp, leaving about a centimetre of paper all around the stamp.

2 Float the stamp, along with others, face down in a shallow dish of water.

3 After about fifteen minutes remove the stamps from the water. With a pair of tweezers, gently peel the stamp from the paper.

4 Place all the stamps on a sheet of blotting paper. When the stamps have dried transfer them to a clean sheet of blotting paper. Place another sheet of blotting paper on top and put a few books on top of that. Leave overnight and the stamps will be ready to stick into your album.

Always use proper stamp hinges to put your stamps in the album.

To become a really expert magician requires a lot of practice, but there are many tricks that are not too difficult to do.

When you are good at doing these simple tricks you can go on to others that are more complicated – perhaps even join a magic club where you will learn even more.

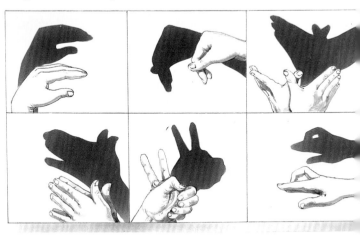

CAST A SHADOW

All you need to make shadow pictures are a good light source and your hands.

With practice you will be able to make the shadows move realistically.

To make your shadow demonstration more interesting for those watching make up a story using the various creatures shown here.

COLOURED THOUGHTS

Tie three differently coloured ribbons together into a loop. Put the ribbons in a paper bag. This is done in secret before you let anyone know you are going to do a trick.

When the time comes to show the trick you hand someone three coloured ribbons and ask him or her to tie them together in any order. These ribbons are the same colours as the ones you put in the bag earlier.

Say you knew which order the ribbons would be tied. To prove this you reach into the bag and remove the three ribbons – and they are in the same order.

To do this you just look at the colours of those at the top and bottom of the three held by the spectator. You then go into your bag and undo the knot that ties the same two colours together.

Bring out the three

ribbons and they are in the same order as those tied by the spectator.

PICK SNAP
A wooden tooth-pick is placed in a handkerchief and broken in two. When the tooth-pick is dropped from the handkerchief it is back in one piece again.

What you do not tell your friends is that you have another tooth-pick hidden in the hem of the handkerchief. It is this secret tooth-pick that is broken and not the one seen by the audience.

SEE IT YOURSELF
Here is a magic trick using three loops of paper. Take three strips of paper, each about a metre long and 5 cm wide. Take the first strip and glue the ends together to form a loop (1a and b). Do the same with the second strip, but give it a complete turn (turn it over and over again) before joining the ends (2a and b). With the third strip, turn one end over once before gluing (3a and b). Now cut the three strips down the centre. The first loop gives you two separate loops (1c). The second forms two linked loops (2c). The third becomes a single loop twice the size of the original (3c)! These magic loops were discovered by Ferdinand Moebius, in 1858.

1 a b c

2 a b c

3 a b c

DO'S AND DON'TS

- Wash your hands before preparing food.

- Keep the kitchen tidy. Wash up utensils and crockery as you finish with them.

- If you have long hair tie it up or wear a hat.

- Wear an apron to keep your clothes clean.

- Do not use the same chopping board for meat and vegetables – unless it has been washed thoroughly between uses.

- Don't guess at weights and measures. Measure items exactly according to the recipe.

Buck Rarebit

Grate 60 grams (2oz) of Cheddar cheese into a pan and melt over a low heat. Add a pinch of mustard and cayenne plus a few drops of Worcester sauce. As cheese is melting, gradually stir in 2 tablespoons of milk.

Poach an egg and toast a slice of bread. Pour mixture over toast and top with an egg.

Scrambled Egg:

Melt a knob of butter in a saucepan. Beat together one egg and one tablespoon of milk and pour into the pan.

Cook gently, stirring continuously until the egg mixture sets.

Pancakes

(For six people):
100 grams (4 oz) flour
2 eggs
1 tablespoon cooking oil
150 ml ($\frac{1}{4}$ pint) milk
2 tablespoons water
pinch of salt

1. Grease the frying pan with oil.
2. Sift the flour into a bowl. Break the eggs into the centre and slowly add milk. Beat well.
3. Add 1 tablespoon water and beat again.
4. Fry a little trial pancake. If the mixture flows too stiffly to form a thin pancake, add another tablespoon of water.
5. Fill a saucepan with hot water, put it on the stove and cover with an upturned plate. Put the cooked pancakes over the plate to keep warm.
6. Fry the pancakes until they are lightly browned on each side.

Fillings for pancakes, pizzas, baked potatoes and omelettes:

Use mushrooms, onions, cucumber, tomato, cooked or grated vegetables, cheese, egg (scrambled or boiled), prawns, chicken, ham, parsley, curry paste, etc.

Coleslaw

Finely chop:
$\frac{1}{4}$ white cabbage
1 small onion
1 large carrot
1 dessert apple

Mix together with salad cream.

Tomato Soup

15 grams ($\frac{1}{2}$ oz) flour
15 grams ($\frac{1}{2}$ oz) butter
300 ml ($\frac{1}{2}$ pint) milk
200 grams (8 oz) tinned tomatoes
Pinch of salt and pepper

Heat the ingredients, stirring continuously. Bring to boil, cover and simmer for 10 minutes.

As a variation, add a chopped onion to the ingredients.

Savoury Fingers

Mix 200 grams (8 oz) plain flour with 75 grams (3 oz) margarine and a pinch of salt until it looks like fine breadcrumbs.

Grate 75 grams (3 oz) hard cheese and add it to the mixture. Add a beaten egg and a teaspoon of milk and mix it all together into a stiff dough.

Sprinkle some flour onto a work surface. Place the dough on the surface and roll it out until it is quite thin.

Cut the dough into short finger-length pieces and place them on a greased baking tray.

Cook in the oven for 20 minutes at 180°C, 350°F, or Gas Mark 4.

Honey Fudge

3 teacups granulated sugar
1½ teacups honey
1 tablespoon water
Cream of tartar
3 egg-whites
50 grams (2 oz) seed-less raisins.

Put the sugar, honey and water into a pan, place over a low heat until the sugar has dissolved. Add a pinch of cream of tartar and boil gently until it forms a soft ball if you put a little into cold water. Leave on a very low heat.

Separate the three egg-whites from the yolks. Put the egg-whites in a medium-sized bowl and whip until they are so stiff that you can turn the basin upside-down. Pour the fudge mixture onto the egg-whites, stir in the raisins, and beat until it becomes thick and creamy. Pour into a greased tin and when almost cold cut into squares. Pack into greaseproof paper.

Cheese Dominoes

25 grams (1 oz) butter
50 grams (2 oz) grated Cheddar cheese
Salt and pepper
Brown bread
Currants

Mix together butter, cheese and salt and pepper. Cut the bread into rectangles.

Spread one side with the cheese mixture. Add the currants to form numbers on the dominoes.

DATAFILE

DATAFILE ON SPORT

ATHLETICS

Men's World Records

100 metres	9.83 sec	Ben Johnson (Canada)	30.8.87
200 metres	19.72 sec	Pietro Mennea (Italy)	12.9.79
400 metres	43.29 sec	'Butch' Reynolds (USA)	17.8.88
800 metres	1 min 41.73 sec	Sebastian Coe (GB)	10.6.81
1000 metres	2 min 12.18 sec	Sebastian Coe (GB)	11.7.81
1500 metres	3 min 29.46 sec	Saïd Aouita (Morocco)	23.8.85
1 mile	3 min 46.32 sec	Steven Cram (GB)	27.7.85
2000 metres	4 min 50.81 sec	Saïd Aouita (Morocco)	16.7.87
3000 metres	7 min 29.45 sec	Saïd Aouita (Morocco)	20.8.89
5000 metres	12 min 58.39 sec	Saïd Aouita (Morocco)	22.7.87
10000 metres	27 min 08.23 sec	Arturo Barrios (Mexico)	18.8.89
Marathon*	2 hr 6 min 50 sec	Belayneh Dinsamo (Ethiopia)	17.4.88
110 metres hurdles	12.92 sec	Roger Kingdom (USA)	16.8.89
400 metres hurdles	47.02 sec	Ed Moses (USA)	31.8.83
3000 m steeplechase	8 min 5.35 sec	Peter Koech (Kenya)	3.7.89
4 x 100 metres relay	37.83 sec	United States	11.8.84
4 x 400 metres relay	2 min 56.16 sec	United States	20.10.68
High jump	2.44 m (7 ft ?? in)	Javier Sotomayor (Cuba)	30.7.89
Pole vault	6.06 m (19ft 10½ in)	Sergey Bubka (USSR)	10.7.88
Long jump	8.90 m (29 ft 2½ in)	Bob Beamon (USA)	18.10.68
Triple jump	17.97 m (58 ft 11 in)	'Willie' Banks (USA)	16.6.85
Shot put	23.06 m (75 ft 8 in)	Ulf Timmerman (E Germany)	22.5.88
Discus throw	74.08 m (243 ft)	Jürgen Schult (E Germany)	6.6.86
Hammer throw	86.74 m (284 ft 7 in)	Yuriy Sedykh (USSR)	30.8.86
Javelin throw†	87.66 m (287 ft 7 in)	Jan Zelezny (Czech)	31.5.87
Decathlon	8847 points	'Daley' Thompson (GB)	8–9.8.84

Women's World Records

100 metres	10.49 sec	Florence Griffith-Joyner (USA)	16.7.88
200 metres	21.34 sec	Florence Griffith-Joyner (USA)	29.9.89
400 metres	47.60 sec	Marita Koch (E Germany)	6.10.85
800 metres	1 min 53.28 sec	Jarmila Kratochvilova (Czech)	26.7.83
1000 metres	2 min 30.60 sec	Tatyana Providokhina (USSR)	20.8.78
1500 metres	3 min 52.47 sec	Tatyana Kazankina (USSR)	13.8.80
1 mile	4 min 15.61 sec	Paula Ivan (Romania)	10.7.89
2000 metres	5 min 28.69 sec	Maricica Puica (Romania)	11.7.86
3000 metres	8 min 22.62 sec	Tatyana Kazankina (USSR)	26.8.84
5000 metres	14 min 37.33 sec	Ingrid Kristiansen (Norway)	5.8.86
10000 metres	30 min 13.74 sec	Ingrid Kristiansen (Norway)	5.7.86
Marathon*	2 hr 21 min 6 sec	Ingrid Kristiansen (Norway)	21.4.85
100 metres hurdles	12.29 sec	Sally Gunnell (GB)	17.8.88
400 metres hurdles	52.94 sec	Marina Styepanova (USSR)	17.9.86
4 x 100 metres relay	41.37 sec	East Germany	6.10.85
4 x 400 metres relay	3 min 15.17 sec	USSR	1.10.88
High jump	2.09 m (6 ft 10¼ in)	Stefka Kostadinova (Bulgaria)	30.8.87
Long jump	7.52 m (24 ft 8¼ in)	Galina Chistyakova (USSR)	11.6.88
Shot put	22.63 m (74 ft 3 in)	Natalya Lisovskaya (USSR)	7.6.87
Discus throw	76.80 m (252 ft)	Gabriele Reinsch (E Germany)	9.7.88
Javelin throw	80.00 m	Petra Felke (E Germany)	9.9.88
Heptathlon	7,291 points	Jackie Joyner-Kersee (USA)	16–17.8.88

*World best time (courses vary)   †New javelin

OLYMPIC GAMES VENUES

I	1896	Athens
II	1900	Paris
III	1904	St Louis
IV	1908	London
V	1912	Stockholm
VI	1916	Berlin*
VII	1920	Antwerp
VIII	1924	Paris
IX	1928	Amsterdam
X	1932	Los Angeles
XI	1936	Berlin
XII	1940	Tokyo, Helsinki*
XIII	1944	London*
XIV	1948	London
XV	1952	Helsinki
XVI	1956	Melbourne
XVII	1960	Rome
XVIII	1964	Tokyo
XIX	1968	Mexico
XX	1972	Munich
XXI	1976	Montreal
XXII	1980	Moscow
XXIII	1984	Los Angeles
XXIV	1988	Seoul
XXV	1992	Barcelona

* = meeting not held because of war

VENUES OF THE WINTER OLYMPICS

I	1924	Chamonix, France
II	1928	St. Moritz, Switzerland
III	1932	Lake Placid, USA
IV	1936	Garmisch-Partenkirchen, West Germany
V	1948	St. Moritz, Switzerland
VI	1952	Oslo, Norway
VII	1956	Cortina, Italy
VIII	1960	Squaw Valley, USA
IX	1964	Innsbruck, Austria
X	1968	Grenoble, France
XI	1972	Sapporo, Japan
XII	1976	Innsbruck, Austria
XIII	1980	Lake Placid, USA
XIV	1984	Sarajevo, Yugoslavia
XV	1988	Calgary, Canada
XVI	1992	Val d'Isère, France

THE DECATHLON

In recent Olympics the Decathlon has proved to be of special interest to the spectators.

The ten events of the modern decathlon have to be contested in the following order:

First day
100 metres
long jump
shot put
high jump
400 metres

Second day
110 metre hurdles
discus
pole-vault
javelin
1500 metres

COMMONWEALTH GAMES

1930 Hamilton, Canada
1934 London, England
1938 Sydney, Australia
1950 Auckland, New Zealand
1954 Vancouver, Canada
1958 Cardiff, Wales
1962 Perth, Australia
1966 Kingston, Jamaica
1970 Edinburgh, Scotland
1974 Christchurch, New Zealand
1978 Edmonton, Canada
1982 Brisbane, Australia
1986 Edinburgh, Scotland
1990 Auckland, New Zealand
1994 Victoria, Canada

EUROPEAN CUP WINNERS

	Men	Women
1965	USSR	USSR
1967	USSR	USSR
1970	East Germany	East Germany
1973	USSR	East Germany
1975	East Germany	East Germany
1977	East Germany	East Germany
1979	East Germany	East Germany
1981	East Germany	East Germany
1983	East Germany	East Germany
1985	USSR	USSR
1987	USSR	East Germany
1989	Great Britain	East Germany

ASSOCIATION FOOTBALL (SOCCER)

WORLD CUP FINALS

Year	Venue	Winner	Score	Runner-up	Score
1930	Montevideo, Uruguay (100,000)*	Uruguay	4	Argentina	2
1934	Rome, Italy (55,000)	Italy	2	Czechoslovakia	1
1938	Paris, France (65,000)	Italy	4	Hungary	2
1950	Rio de Janeiro, Brazil (199,850)	Uruguay	2	Brazil	1
1954	Berne, Switzerland (55,000)	W Germany	3	Hungary	2
1958	Stockholm, Sweden (49,000)	Brazil	5	Sweden	2
1962	Santiago, Chile (69,500)	Brazil	3	Czechoslovakia	1
1966	Wembley, England (93,000)	England	4	W Germany	2
1970	Mexico City, Mexico (110,000)	Brazil	4	Italy	1
1974	Munich, W Germany (75,000)	W Germany	2	Netherlands	1
1978	Buenos Aires, Argentina (77,000)	Argentina	3	Netherlands	1
1982	Madrid, Spain (90,000)	Italy	3	W Germany	1
1986	Mexico City, Mexico (114,580)	Argentina	3	W Germany	2
1990	Rome, Italy	W Germany	1	Argentina	0

*Number of spectators

EUROPEAN CUP FINALS

Year	Venue	Winner	Score	Runner-up	Score
1956	Paris	Real Madrid (Spain)	4	Stade de Reims (France)	3
1957	Madrid	Real Madrid (Spain)	2	Fiorentina (Italy)	0
1958	Brussels	Real Madrid (Spain)	3	AC Milan (Italy)	2
1959	Stuttgart	Real Madrid (Spain)	2	Stade de Reims (France)	0
1960	Glasgow	Real Madrid (Spain)	7	Eintracht Frankfurt (W Ger)	3
1961	Berne	Benfica (Portugal)	3	Barcelona (Spain)	2
1962	Amsterdam	Benfica (Portugal)	5	Real Madrid (Spain)	3
1963	Wembley	AC Milan (Italy)	2	Benfica (Portugal)	1
1964	Vienna	Internazionale (Italy)	3	Real Madrid (Spain)	1
1965	Milan	Internazionale (Italy)	1	Benfica (Portugal)	0
1966	Brussels	Real Madrid (Spain)	2	Partizan Belgrade (Yug)	1
1967	Lisbon	Celtic (Scotland)	2	Internazionale (Italy)	1
1968	Wembley	Manchester United (England)	4	Benfica (Portugal)	1
1969	Madrid	AC Milan (Italy)	4	Ajax (Netherlands)	1
1970	Milan	Feyenoord (Netherlands)	2	Celtic (Scotland)	1
1971	Wembley	Ajax (Netherlands)	2	Panathinaikos (Greece)	0
1972	Rotterdam	Ajax (Netherlands)	2	Internazionale (Italy)	0
1973	Belgrade	Ajax (Netherlands)	1	Juventus (Italy)	0
1974	Brussels	Bayern Munich (W Ger)	1	Atlético Madrid (Spain)	1
	Replay	Bayern Munich (W Ger)	4	Atlético Madrid (Spain)	0
1975	Paris	Bayern Munich (W Ger)	2	Leeds United (England)	0
1976	Glasgow	Bayern Munich (W Ger)	1	St Etienne (France)	0
1977	Rome	Liverpool (England)	3	B Mönchengladbach (W Ger)	1
1978	Wembley	Liverpool (England)	1	FC Bruges (Belgium)	0
1979	Munich	Nottingham Forest (England)	1	Malmö (Sweden)	0
1980	Madrid	Nottingham Forest (England)	1	SV Hamburg (W Ger)	0
1981	Paris	Liverpool (England)	1	Real Madrid (Spain)	0
1982	Rotterdam	Aston Villa (England)	1	Bayern Munich (W Ger)	0
1983	Athens	Hamburg (W Ger)	1	Juventus (Italy)	0
1984	Rome	Liverpool (England)	1	AS Roma (Italy)	1
	(Liverpool won 4–2 on penalties)				
1985	Brussels	Juventus (Italy)	1	Liverpool (England)	0
1986	Seville	Steaua Bucharest (Romania)	0	Barcelona (Spain)	0
	(Steaua won 2–0 on penalties)				
1987	Vienna	FC Porto (Portugal)	2	Bayern Munich (W Ger)	1
1988	Stuttgart	PSV Eindhoven (Netherlands)	0	Benfica (Portugal)	0
	(Eindhoven won 6–5 on penalties)				
1989	Barcelona	AC Milan (Italy)	4	Steaua Bucharest (Romania)	0

FA CUP WINNERS

1930 Arsenal	1963 Manchester United
1931 West Bromwich Albion	1964 West Ham United
1932 Newcastle United	1965 Liverpool
1933 Everton	1966 Everton
1934 Manchester City	1967 Tottenham Hotspur
1935 Sheffield Wednesday	1968 West Bromwich Albion
1936 Arsenal	1969 Manchester City
1937 Sunderland	1970 Chelsea
1938 Preston North End	1971 Arsenal
1939 Portsmouth	1972 Leeds United
1946 Derby County	1973 Sunderland
1947 Charlton Athletic	1974 Liverpool
1948 Manchester United	1975 West Ham United
1949 Wolverhampton Wanderers	1976 Southampton
1950 Arsenal	1977 Manchester United
1951 Newcastle United	1978 Ipswich Town
1952 Newcastle United	1979 Arsenal
1953 Blackpool	1980 West Ham United
1954 West Bromwich Albion	1981 Tottenham Hotspur
1955 Newcastle United	1982 Tottenham Hotspur
1956 Manchester City	1983 Manchester United
1957 Aston Villa	1984 Everton
1958 Bolton Wanderers	1985 Manchester United
1959 Nottingham Forest	1986 Liverpool
1960 Wolverhampton Wanderers	1987 Coventry City
1961 Tottenham Hotspur	1988 Wimbledon
1962 Tottenham Hotspur	1989 Liverpool
	1990 Manchester United

AMERICAN FOOTBALL SUPER BOWL RESULTS

Year	Field	Winner	Loser
1967	Los Angeles Coliseum	Green Bay Packers 35	Kansas City Chiefs 10
1968	Orange Bowl, Miami	Green Bay Packers 33	Oakland Raiders 14
1969	Orange Bowl, Miami	New York Jets 16	Baltimore Colts.........7
1970	Tulane Stadium, New Orleans	Kansas City Chiefs 23	Minnesota Vikings......7
1971	Orange Bowl, Miami	Baltimore Colts........16	Dallas Cowboys.......13
1972	Tulane Stadium, New Orleans	Dallas Cowboys........24	Miami Dolphins 3
1973	Los Angeles Coliseum	Miami Dolphins 14	Washington Redskins..7
1974	Rice Stadium, Houston	Miami Dolphins 24	Minnesota Vikings......7
1975	Tulane Stadium, New Orleans	Pittsburgh Steelers....16	Minnesota Vikings......6
1976	Orange Bowl, Miami	Pittsburgh Steelers....21	Dallas Cowboys........17
1977	Rose Bowl, Pasadena	Oakland Raiders 32	Minnesota Vikings......14
1978	Superdome, New Orleans	Dallas Cowboys........27	Denver Broncos 10
1979	Orange Bowl, Miami	Pittsburgh Steelers....35	Dallas Cowboys........31
1980	Rose Bowl, Pasadena	Pittsburgh Steelers....31	Los Angeles Rams 19
1981	Superdome, New Orleans	Oakland Raiders 27	Philadelphia Eagles 10
1982	Silverdome, Pontiac, Michigan	San Francisco 49ers ...26	Cincinatti Bengals 21
1983	Rose Bowl, Pasadena	Washington Redskins.27	Miami Dolphins 17
1984	Tampa Stadium	Los Angeles Raiders...38	Washington Redskins..9
1985	Stanford Stadium	San Francisco 49ers ...38	Miami Dolphins 16
1986	Superdome, New Orleans	Chicago Bears 46	New England Patriots 10
1987	Rose Bowl, Pasadena	New York Giants......39	Denver Broncos 20
1988	Sandiego Stadium	Washington Redskins.42	Denver Broncos 10
1989	Joe Robbie Stadium, Miami	San Francisco 49ers ...20	Cincinnati Bengals.....16
1990	Superdome, New Orleans	San Francisco 49ers......55	Denver Broncos............10

CRICKET RECORDS
– ALL MATCHES

Highest innings 499 Hanif Mohammad, Karachi (v Bahawalpur, 1959)
Most runs in season 3,816 D C S Compton, England and Middlesex, 1947; in career 61,237 J B Hobbs, England and Surrey
Most hundreds in career 197 J B Hobbs, England and Surrey
Most runs in over 36 G S Sobers, Nottinghamshire (v Glamorgan, Swansea, 1968) and R J Shastri, Bombay (v Baroda, India, 1985)
Best bowling in innings 10–10 H Verity, Yorkshire (v Nottinghamshire, Leeds, 1932)
Most wickets in season 304 A P Freeman, England and Kent, 1928; in career 4,187 W Rhodes, England and Yorkshire
Highest partnership 577 (4th wkt) V S Hazare (288) and Gul Mahomed (319), Baroda (v Holkar, Baroda, 1947)
Highest total 1,107 (all out) Victoria (v NSW, Melbourne, 1926)
Most wicket-keeping dismissals in career 1,648 R W Taylor, England and Derbyshire

CRICKET RECORDS
– TEST MATCHES

Highest innings 365* G S Sobers, W Indies (v Pakistan, Kingston, 1958)
Most runs in series 974 D G Bradman, Australia (v England, 1930)
in career – 10,122 S Gavaskar, India
Most hundreds in career 34 S Gavaskar, India
Best bowling in match 19–90 J C Laker, England (v Aus., Old Trafford, 1956)
in innings – 10–53 J C Laker, England (v Australia, Old Trafford, 1956)
Most wickets in series 49 S F Barnes, England (v S Africa, 1913–14)
in career 395 R J Hadlee, New Zealand
Highest partnership 451 (2nd wkt) W H Ponsford (266) & D G Bradman (244), Australia (v England, Oval, 1934)
Highest total 903 (for 7) England (v Australia, Oval, 1938)
Most wicket-keeping dismissals in career 355 R W Marsh, Australia
Most Test appearances 125 S Gavaskar, India

RUGBY UNION
International championship since 1970

Year	Winners
1958	England
1959	France
1960	France and England
1961	France
1962	France
1963	England
1964	Scotland and Wales
1965	Wales
1966	Wales
1967	France
1968	France
1969	Wales
1970	Wales and France
1971	Wales
1972	–
1973	All five countries finished level
1974	Ireland
1975	Wales
1976	Wales
1977	France
1978	Wales
1979	Wales
1980	England
1981	France
1982	Ireland
1983	France and Ireland
1984	Scotland
1985	Ireland
1986	France and Scotland
1987	France
1988	Wales and France
1989	France
1990	Scotland

TEST MATCHES
(in the 1980s)

Country	Played	Won
Australia	94	26
England	104	20
India	77	11
New Zealand	59	17
Pakistan	77	23
Sri Lanka	27	2
West Indies	82	44

WIMBLEDON CHAMPIONS
(since 1946)

	Men	Women
1946	Yvon Petra (Fr)	Pauline Betz (US)
1947	Jack Kramer (US)	Margaret Osborne (US)
1948	Bob Falkenburg (US)	Louise Brough (US)
1949	Fred Schroeder (US)	Louise Brough (US)
1950	Budge Patty (US)	Louise Brough (US)
1951	Dick Savitt (US)	Doris Hart (US)
1952	Frank Sedgman (Aus)	Maureen Connolly (US)
1953	Victor Seixas (US)	Maureen Connolly (US)
1954	Jaroslav Drobny (Czech)	Maureen Connolly (US)
1955	Tony Trabert (US)	Louise Brough (US)
1956	Lew Hoad (Aus)	Shirley Fry (US)
1957	Lew Hoad (Aus)	Althea Gibson (US)
1958	Ashley Cooper (Aus)	Althea Gibson (US)
1959	Alex Olmedo (Peru)	Maria Bueno (Brazil)
1960	Neale Fraser (Aus)	Maria Bueno (Brazil)
1961	Rod Laver (Aus)	Angela Mortimer (GB)
1962	Rod Laver (Aus)	Karen Susman (US)
1963	Chuck McKinley (US)	Margaret Smith (Aus)
1964	Roy Emerson (Aus)	Maria Bueno (Brazil)
1965	Roy Emerson (Aus)	Margaret Smith (Aus)
1966	Manuel Santana (Sp)	Billie Jean King (US)
1967	John Newcombe (Aus)	Billie Jean King (US)
1968	Rod Laver (Aus)	Billie Jean King (US)
1969	Rod Laver (Aus)	Ann Jones (GB)
1970	John Newcombe (Aus)	Margaret Court* (Aus)
1971	John Newcombe (Aus)	Evonne Goolagong (Aus)
1972	Stan Smith (US)	Billie Jean King (US)
1973	Jan Kodes (Czech)	Billie Jean King (US)
1974	Jimmy Connors (US)	Chris Evert (US)
1975	Arthur Ashe (US)	Billie Jean King (US)
1976	Bjorn Borg (Swed)	Chris Evert (US)
1977	Bjorn Borg (Swed)	Virginia Wade (GB)
1978	Bjorn Borg (Swed)	Martina Navratilova (Czech)
1979	Bjorn Borg (Swed)	Martina Navratilova (Czech)
1980	Bjorn Borg (Swed)	Evonne Cawley† (Aus)
1981	John McEnroe (US)	Chris Evert-Lloyd (US)
1982	Jimmy Connors (US)	Martina Navratilova (US)
1983	John McEnroe (US)	Martina Navratilova (US)
1984	John McEnroe (US)	Martina Navratilova (US)
1985	Boris Becker (W Ger)	Martina Navratilova (US)
1986	Boris Becker (W Ger)	Martina Navratilova (US)
1987	Pat Cash (Aus)	Martina Navratilova (US)
1988	Stefan Edberg (Swed)	Steffi Graf (W Ger)
1989	Boris Becker (W Ger)	Steffi Graf (W Ger)
1990	Stefan Edberg (Swed)	Martina Navratilova (US)

Boris Becker, three times winner of the men's single at Wimbledon.

Steffi Graf, women's singles winner at Wimbledon in 1988 and 1989.

*Formerly Margaret Smith
†Formerly Evonne Goolagong

DATAFILE ON COUNTRIES

AFRICA

Country	Area sq km	Population	Capital	Official language
Algeria	2,378,896	22,800,000	Algiers	Arabic
Angola	1,246,700	8,200,000	Luanda	Portuguese
Benin	112,620	4,100,000	Porto Novo	French
Botswana	600,370	1,100,000	Gaborone	English, Setswana
Burkina Faso	274,200	7,100,000	Ouagadougou	French
Burundi	27,836	4,800,000	Bujumbura	French, Kirundi
Cameroon	480,620	10,000,000	Yaoundé	English, French
Cape Verde	4,532	318,000	Praia	Portuguese
Central African Republic	622,980	2,700,000	Bangui	French
Chad	1,284,000	5,200,000	N'Djamena	French
Comoros	2,170	420,000	Moroni	French
Congo	342,000	1,900,000	Brazzaville	French
Côte d'Ivoire	322,460	10,500,000	Abidjan	French
Djibouti	22,000	300,000	Djibouti	French
Egypt	1,001,420	50,500,000	Cairo	Arabic
Equatorial Guinea	28,055	360,000	Malabo	Spanish
Ethiopia	1,221,894	43,900,000	Addis Ababa	Amharic
Gabon	267,665	1,000,000	Libreville	French
Gambia	11,295	800,000	Banjul	English
Ghana	238,537	13,500,000	Accra	English
Guinea	245,976	5,700,000	Conakry	French
Guinea-Bissau	36,125	900,000	Bissau	Portuguese
Kenya	582,644	21,000,000	Nairobi	English, Swahili
Lesotho	30,344	1,500,000	Maseru	English, Sesotho
Liberia	99,067	2,300,000	Monrovia	English
Libya	1,759,532	4,000,000	Tripoli	Arabic
Madagascar	587,040	10,200,000	Antananarivo	French, Malagasy
Malawi	118,484	7,300,000	Lilongwe	English, Chichewa
Mali	1,240,000	7,900,000	Bamako	French
Mauritania	1,030,700	1,700,000	Nouakchott	Arabic, French
Mauritius	2,046	1,000,000	Port Louis	English
Morocco	446,547	23,700,000	Rabat	Arabic
Mozambique	801,560	14,000,000	Maputo	Portuguese
Namibia	824,292	1,100,000	Windhoek	Afrikaans, English
Niger	1,267,000	6,700,000	Niamey	French
Nigeria	923,763	105,400,000	Lagos	English
Rwanda	26,338	6,500,000	Kigali	French, Kinyarwanda
São Tomé and Príncipe	963	108,000	São Tomé	Portuguese
Senegal	196,192	70,000	Dakar	French
Seychelles	443	167,000	Victoria	English, French
Sierra Leone	71,740	4,000,000	Freetown	English
Somali Republic	637,914	7,800,000	Mogadishu	Somali
South Africa	1,223,404	33,200,000	Pretoria (seat of government); Cape Town (legal capital)	Afrikaans, English
Sudan	2,503,900	22,900,000	Khartoum	Arabic

AFRICA – continued

Swaziland	17,363	690,000	Mbabane	English
Tanzania	945,050	22,400,000	Dodoma	English, Swahili
Togo	56,000	3,100,000	Lomé	French
Tunisia	163,610	7,400,000	Tunis	Arabic
Uganda	241,785	15,200,000	Kampala	English
Zaïre	2,345,400	31,300,000	Kinshasa	French
Zambia	752,614	7,000,000	Lusaka	English
Zimbabwe	390,580	9,000,000	Harare	English

ASIA

Country	Area sq km	Population	Capital	Official language
Afghanistan	652,090	15,000,000	Kabul	Pashtu, Dari
Bahrain	668	440,000	Manama	Arabic
Bangladesh	143,998	104,200,000	Dhaka	Bengali
Bhutan	47,000	1,400,000	Thimphu	Dzongkha
Brunei	5,765	240,000	Bandar Seri Begawar	Malay
Burma (renamed the Union of Myanamar in 1989)	678,030	37,600,000	Rangoon (renamed Yangon)	Burmese
Cambodia	181,035	6,400,000	Phnom Penh	Khmer
China	9,596,915	1,045,500,000	Beijing	Chinese (Mandarin)
Cyprus	9,250	700,000	Nicosia	Greek, Turkish
India	3,280,466	783,900,000	Delhi	Hindi, English
Indonesia	1,904,335	176,800,000	Jakarta	Bahasa (Indonesian)
Iran	1,647,990	46,600,000	Teheran	Persian (Farsi)
Iraq	434,920	16,000,000	Baghdad	Arabic
Israel	29,324	4,200,000	Jerusalem	Hebrew, Arabic
Japan	377,765	121,400,000	Tokyo	Japanese
Jordan	97,738	2,800,000	Amman	Arabic
Korea, North	120,538	20,500,000	Pyongyang	Korean
Korea, South	98,484	43,300,000	Seoul	Korean
Kuwait	17,820	1,800,000	Al Kuwait	Arabic
Laos	236,797	3,700,000	Vientiane	Lao
Lebanon	10,400	2,600,000	Beirut	Arabic
Malaysia	330,868	15,800,000	Kuala Lumpur	Malay
Maldives	298	180,000	Malé	Divehi
Mongolia	1,564,992	1,900,000	Ulan Bator	Mongol
Nepal	145,392	17,400,000	Katmandu	Nepali
Oman	212,457	1,300,000	Muscat	Arabic
Pakistan	803,940	101,800,000	Islamabad	Urdu
Philippines	300,000	58,100,000	Manila	English, Philipino
Qatar	11,000	305,000	Doha	Arabic
Saudi Arabia	2,175,580	11,500,000	Riyadh	Arabic
Singapore	580	2,600,000	Singapore	Malay, Chinese, Tamil, English
Sri Lanka	65,610	16,600,000	Colombo	Sinhala
Syria	185,180	10,900,000	Damascus	Arabic
Taiwan	35,962	19,600,000	Taipei	Chinese (Mandarin)
Thailand	514,000	52,400,000	Bangkok	Thai
Turkey	780,573	51,800,000	Ankara	Turkish

United Arab Emirates	82,900	1,300,000	Abu Dhabi	Arabic
Vietnam	332,557	62,000,000	Hanoi	Vietnamese
Republic of Yemen	527,966	9,430,000	San'a	Arabic

EUROPE

Country	Area sq km	Population	Capital	Official language
Albania	28,750	3,000,000	Tirana	Albanian
Andorra	486	49,000	Andorra la Vella	Catalan
Austria	83,850	7,500,000	Vienna	German
Belgium	30,507	9,900,000	Brussels	Flemish, French
Bulgaria	110,910	8,900,000	Sofia	Bulgarian
Czechoslovakia	127,855	15,500,000	Prague	Czech
Denmark	43,080	5,100,000	Copenhagen	Danish
Finland	337,006	4,900,000	Helsinki	Finnish, Swedish
France	572,923	55,000,000	Paris	French
Germany, East	108,178	16,700,000	East Berlin	German
Germany, West	248,574	61,000,000	Bonn	German
Greece	132,467	10,100,000	Athens	Greek
Hungary	93,030	10,800,000	Budapest	Hungarian
Iceland	103,053	244,000	Reykjavik	Icelandic
Ireland, Republic of	70,284	3,600,000	Dublin	English, Irish
Italy	301,223	57,400,000	Rome	Italian
Liechtenstein	160	28,000	Vaduz	German
Luxembourg	2,585	400,000	Luxembourg City	French, Luxemburgish
Malta	316	400,000	Valletta	Maltese, English
Monaco	1.6	28,000	Monaco	French
Netherlands	40,844	14,500,000	Amsterdam; The Hague is the seat of government	Dutch
Norway	324,217	4,200,000	Oslo	Norwegian
Poland	312,680	37,500,000	Warsaw	Polish
Portugal	92,082	10,400,000	Lisbon	Portuguese
Romania	237,500	22,800,000	Bucharest	Romanian
San Marino	62	23,000	San Marino	Italian
Spain	504,728	39,000,000	Madrid	Spanish
Sweden	449,960	8,300,000	Stockholm	Swedish
Switzerland	41,287	6,500,000	Bern	French, German, Italian
United Kingdom	244,044	56,400,000	London	English
USSR	22,402,090	280,000,000	Moscow	Russian
Vatican City State	0.44	1,000	Vatican City	Italian, Latin
Yugoslavia	255,803	23,300,000	Belgrade	Serbo-Croat, Slovene, Macedonian

NORTH & CENTRAL AMERICA

Country	Area sq km	Population	Capital	Official language
Antigua and Barbuda	443	82,000	St. John's	English
Bahamas	13,934	240,000	Nassau	English
Barbados	430	250,000	Bridgetown	English
Belize	22,965	170,000	Belmopan	English, Spanish
Canada	9,976,090	25,600,000	Ottawa	English, French
Costa Rica	50,700	2,700,000	San José	Spanish
Cuba	114,524	10,200,000	Havana	Spanish
Dominica	750	74,000	Roseau	English
Dominican Republic	48,733	6,800,000	Santo Domingo	Spanish
El Salvador	21,393	510,000	San Salvador	Spanish
Grenada	344	86,000	St. George's	English
Guatemala	108,888	8,600,000	Guatemala City	Spanish
Haiti	27,750	5,800,000	Port-au-Prince	French
Honduras	112,087	4,600,000	Tegucigalpa	Spanish
Jamaica	10,960	2,300,000	Kingston	English
Mexico	1,972,545	81,700,000	Mexico City	Spanish
Nicaragua	130,000	3,300,000	Managua	Spanish
Panama	75,648	2,200,000	Panama	Spanish
Saint Christopher (St Kitts) and Nevis	262	40,000	Basseterre	English
Saint Lucia	616	120,000	Castries	English
Saint Vincent and the Grenadines	388	100,000	Kingstown	English
Trinidad and Tobago	5,128	1,200,000	Port-of-Spain	English
United States of America	9,372,570	240,800,000	Washington D.C.	English

A coffee plant, showing the beans. In Brazil and Colombia coffee is an important export.

SOUTH AMERICA

Country	Area sq km	Population	Capital	Official language
Argentina	2,758,826	31,100,000	Buenos Aires	Spanish
Bolivia	1,098,582	6,200,000	La Paz (seat of government); Sucre (legal capital)	Spanish
Brazil	8,511,917	143,300,000	Brasilia	Portuguese
Chile	756,942	12,300,000	Santiago	Spanish
Colombia	1,138,908	30,000,000	Bogotá	Spanish
Ecuador	283,560	9,700,000	Quito	Spanish
Guyana	214,970	770,000	Georgetown	English
Paraguay	406,750	4,100,000	Asunción	Spanish
Peru	1,277,440	20,200,000	Lima	Spanish
Surinam	163,265	380,000	Paramaribo	Dutch, English
Uruguay	176,215	3,000,000	Montevideo	Spanish
Venezuela	912,046	17,800,000	Caracas	Spanish

OCEANIA

Country	Area sq km	Population	Capital	Official Language
Australia	7,682,422	15,800,000	Canberra	English
Fiji	18,275	700,000	Suva	English, Fijian
Kiribati	689	63,000	Tarawa	English, Gilbertese
Nauru	21	8,000	Nauru	English, Nauruan
New Zealand	268,675	3,300,000	Wellington	English
Papua New Guinea	461,687	3,400,000	Port Moresby	English
Solomon Islands	27,557	300,000	Honiara	English
Tonga	700	100,000	Nuku'alofa	English
Tuvalu	26	8,500	Fongafale	English, Tuvalu
Vanuatu	14,763	136,000	Port Vila	Bislama, English, French
Western Samoa	2,934	200,000	Apia	English, Samoan

PROVINCES AND TERRITORIES OF CANADA

Province or territory	Capital
Alberta	Edmonton
British Columbia	Victoria
Manitoba	Winnipeg
New Brunswick	Fredericton
Newfoundland	St John's
Northwest Territory	Yellowknife
Nova Scotia	Halifax
Ontario	Toronto
Prince Edward Is.	Charlottetown
Quebec	Quebec
Saskatchewan	Regina
Yukon Territory	Whitehorse

The church of St Basil in Red Square, Moscow. Right: The Capitol Building, Washington DC, USA.

STATES AND TERRITORIES OF AUSTRALIA

State or territory	Capital
Australian Capital Territory	Canberra
New South Wales	Sydney
Northern Territory	Darwin
Queensland	Brisbane
South Australia	Adelaide
Tasmania	Hobart
Victoria	Melbourne
Western Australia	Perth

REPUBLICS OF THE USSR

Republic	Capital
Armenia	Yerevan
Azerbaijan	Baku
Belorussia	Minsk
Estonia	Tallinn
Georgia	Tbilisi
Kazakhastan	Alma-Ata
Kirgizia	Frunze
Latvia	Riga
Lithuania*	Vilnius
Moldavia	Kishinev
Russian SFSR	Moscow
Tadzhikistan	Dushanbe
Turkmenistan	Ashkhabac
Ukraine	Kiev
Uzbekistan	Tashkent

*Voted for independence from USSR in March 1990.

THE STATES OF THE USA

State	Capital	State	Capital
Alabama	Montgomery	Montana	Helena
Alaska	Juneau	Nebraska	Lincoln
Arizona	Phoenix	Nevada	Carson City
Arkansas	Little Rock	New Hampshire	Concord
California	Sacramento	New Jersey	Trenton
Colorado	Denver	New Mexico	Santa Fe
Connecticut	Hartford	New York	Albany
Delaware	Dover	North Carolina	Raleigh
Florida	Tallahassee	North Dakota	Bismarck
Georgia	Atlanta	Ohio	Columbus
Hawaii	Honolulu	Oklahoma	Oklahoma City
Idaho	Boise	Oregon	Salem
Illinois	Springfield	Pennsylvania	Harrisburg
Indiana	Indianapolis	Rhode Island	Providence
Iowa	Des Moines	South Carolina	Columbia
Kansas	Topeka	South Dakota	Pierre
Kentucky	Frankfort	Tennessee	Nashville
Louisiana	Baton Rouge	Texas	Austin
Maine	Augusta	Utah	Salt Lake City
Maryland	Annapolis	Vermont	Montpelier
Massachusetts	Boston	Virginia	Richmond
Michigan	Lansing	Washington	Olympia
Minnesota	St Paul	West Virginia	Charleston
Mississippi	Jackson	Wisconsin	Madison
Missouri	Jefferson City	Wyoming	Cheyenne

UNITED KINGDOM ADMINISTRATIVE AREAS

England – counties
Avon
Bedfordshire
Berkshire
Buckinghamshire
Cambridgeshire
Cheshire
Cleveland
Cornwall
Cumbria
Derbyshire
Devon
Dorset
Durham
East Sussex
Essex
Gloucestershire
Greater London
Greater Manchester
Hampshire

Hereford
   & Worcester
Hertfordshire
Humberside
Isle of Wight
Isles of Scilly
Kent
Lancashire
Leicestershire
Lincolnshire
Merseyside
Norfolk
Northamptonshire
Northumberland
North Yorkshire
Nottinghamshire
Oxfordshire
Shropshire
Somerset
South Yorkshire

Staffordshire
Suffolk
Surrey
Tyne & Wear
Warwickshire
West Midlands
West Sussex
West Yorkshire
Wiltshire

Wales – counties
Clwyd
Dyfed
Gwent
Gwynedd
Mid Glamorgan
Powys
South Glamorgan
West Glamorgan

Scotland – *regions*
Borders
Central
Dumfries & Galloway
Fife
Grampian
Highland
Lothian
Strathclyde
Tayside

Island areas
Orkney; Shetland
Western Isles

N. Ireland – *counties*
Antrim; Armagh
Down; Fermanagh
Londonderry
Tyrone

FLAGS OF THE WORLD

Afghanistan

Austria

Bhutan

Burundi

Albania

Bahamas

Bolivia

Cambodia

Algeria

Bahrain

Botswana

Cameroon

Andorra

Bangladesh

Brazil

Canada

Angola

Barbados

Brunei

Central African Republic

Antigua and Barbuda

Belgium

Bulgaria

Chad

Argentina

Belize

Burkina Faso

Chile

Australia

Benin

Burma

China

The blue, white and red of the French tricolour are said to stand for Liberty, Equality and Fraternity.

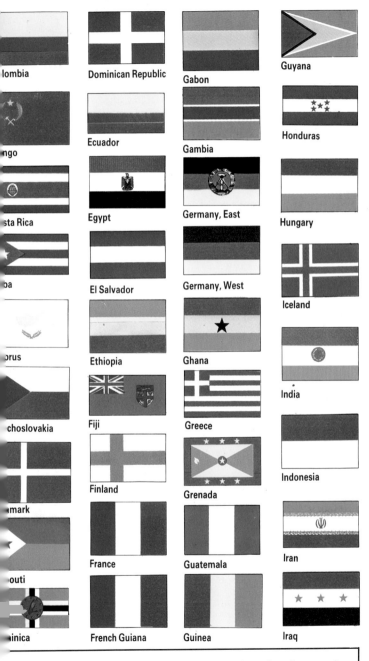

lombia

Dominican Republic

Gabon

Guyana

ngo

Ecuador

Gambia

Honduras

sta Rica

Egypt

Germany, East

Hungary

ba

El Salvador

Germany, West

Iceland

rus

Ethiopia

Ghana

India

choslovakia

Fiji

Greece

Indonesia

mark

Finland

Grenada

Iran

outi

France

Guatemala

inica

French Guiana

Guinea

Iraq

All the flags of Scandinavia are based on the 'Scandinavian cross' in which the fly-end arm is longer than the one at the hoist.

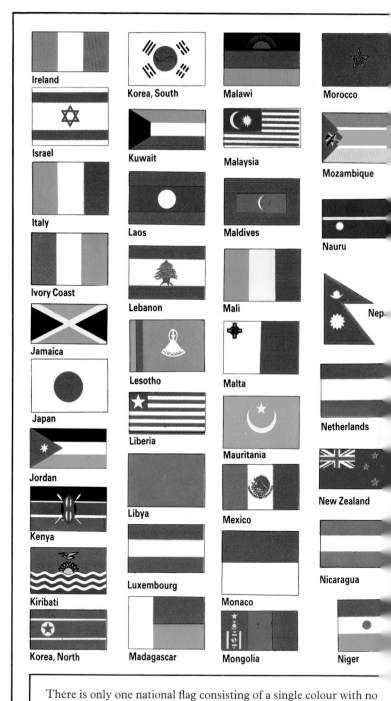

Ireland

Korea, South

Malawi

Morocco

Israel

Kuwait

Malaysia

Mozambique

Italy

Laos

Maldives

Nauru

Ivory Coast

Lebanon

Mali

Nepal

Jamaica

Lesotho

Malta

Japan

Liberia

Netherlands

Jordan

Mauritania

Libya

Mexico

New Zealand

Kenya

Luxembourg

Nicaragua

Kiribati

Madagascar

Monaco

Korea, North

Mongolia

Niger

There is only one national flag consisting of a single colour with no
emblems and that is the all-green flag of Libya.

170

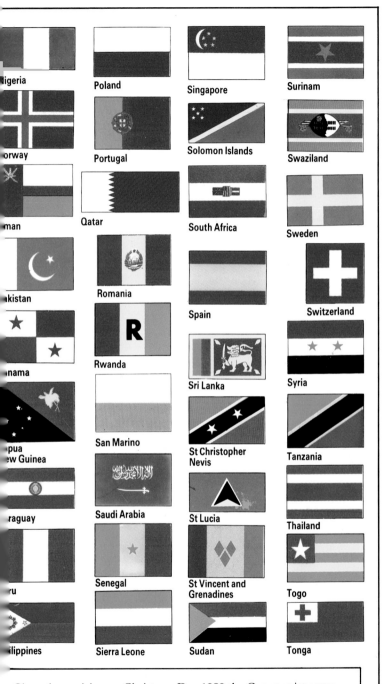

Nigeria

Poland

Singapore

Surinam

Norway

Portugal

Solomon Islands

Swaziland

Oman

Qatar

South Africa

Sweden

Pakistan

Romania

Spain

Switzerland

Panama

R

Rwanda

Sri Lanka

Syria

Papua New Guinea

San Marino

St Christopher Nevis

Tanzania

Paraguay

Saudi Arabia

St Lucia

Thailand

Peru

Senegal

St Vincent and Grenadines

Togo

Philippines

Sierra Leone

Sudan

Tonga

Since the uprising on Christmas Day 1989 the Communist arms have been dropped from the Romanian flag.

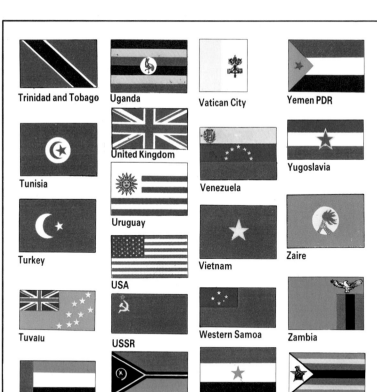

Trinidad and Tobago Uganda Vatican City Yemen PDR

Tunisia United Kingdom Venezuela Yugoslavia

Uruguay

Turkey USA Vietnam Zaire

Tuvalu USSR Western Samoa Zambia

UAE
(United Arab Emirates) Vanuatu Yemen AR Zimbabwe

THE UNITED NATIONS

The United Nations Organization was created officially on 24 October, 1945 to maintain international peace and security.

It is divided into six principal working groups:

The General Assembly consisting of all member nations, the delegates of which meet annually and on special occasions at the United Nations headquarters in New York.

The Security Council which is primarily responsible for international peace and comprises 15 member countries.

The Economic and Social Council which deals with economic, social, educational, health and cultural matters.

The International Court of Justice, composed of 15 judges who meet at The Hague to consider international disputes and advise on international law.

The Secretariat, the administrative section of the United Nations.

The Trusteeship Council which administers countries which were colonies of other countries until such time as they are capable of ruling themselves.

SECRETARY GENERALS OF THE UNITED NATIONS

Trygve Lie	1946–53
Norway	
Dag Hammarskjöld	1953–61
Sweden	
U Thant	1961–72
Burma	
Kurt Waldheim	1972–82
Austria	
Javier Pérez de Cuellar	1982–
Peru	

AGENCIES OF THE UNITED NATIONS

FAO	Food and Agriculture Organization	ILO	International Labour Organization
IBRD	International Bank for Reconstruction and Development	IMF	International Monetary Fund
ICAO	International Civil Aviation Organization	IMO	International Maritime Organization
IDO	International Development Organization	ITU	International Telecommunications Union
IFAD	International Fund for Agricultural Development	UNESCO	United Nations Education, Scientific and Cultural Organization
IFC	International Finance Corporation	UPU	Universal Postal Union
		WHO	World Health Organization
		WMO	World Meteorological Organization

THE COMMONWEALTH OF NATIONS

This is a voluntary association of independent states. The Head of the Commonwealth is HM Queen Elizabeth II. Present members of the Commonwealth (with date of independence in brackets) are: Antigua & Barbuda (1981), Australia (1901), Bahamas (1973), Bangladesh: (from Pakistan, 1971), Barbados (1966), Belize (1981), Botswana (1966), Brunei (1984), Canada (1931), Cyprus (1960), Dominica (1978), The Gambia (1965), Ghana (1957), Great Britain, Grenada (1974), Guyana (1966), India (1947), Jamaica (1962), Kenya (1963), Kiribati (1979), Lesotho (1966), Malawi (1964), Malaysia (1957), Maldives (1965), Malta (1964), Mauritius (1968), Nauru (1968), New Zealand (1907), Nigeria (1960), Papua New Guinea (1975), St Kitts-Nevis (1983), St Lucia (1979), St Vincent (1979), Seychelles (1976), Sierra Leone (1961), Singapore (1965), Solomon Islands (1978), Sri Lanka (1948), Swaziland (1968), Tanzania (1961), Tonga (1970), Trinidad & Tobago (1962), Tuvalu (1978), Uganda (1962), Vanuatu (1980), Western Somoa (1962), Zambia (1964), Zimbabwe (1980).

The emblem of the UN.

THE EUROPEAN COMMUNITY

The European (Economic) Community (EEC or EC) originated in 1955 when the six members of the European Coal and Steel Community agreed to widen the scope of co-operation between their countries. In 1957 The Treaty of Rome set out the main aims of the EC and it came formally into being in January, 1958. There are now 12 countries who are members of the EC: Belgium, Denmark, France, Federal Republic of Germany, Greece, Ireland, Italy, Luxembourg, The Netherlands, Portugal, Spain, United Kingdom.

INTERNATIONAL ORGANIZATIONS

ASEAN	Association of South-East Asian Nations	OAS	Organization of American States
COMECON	Council for Mutual Economic Aid	OAU	Organization of African Unity
EEC	European Economic Community also known as European Community (EC)	OECD	Organization for Economic Development and Co-operation
EFTA	European Free Trade Association	OPEC	Organization of Petroleum-Exporting Countries
NATO	North Atlantic Treaty Organization	UN(O)	United Nations (Organization)

DATAFILE ON THE EARTH

AVERAGE DISTANCE

Planet	from Sun (million km)	Diameter km
Mercury	57.9	4,880
Venus	108.2	12,100
Earth	149.6	12,756
Mars	227.9	6,790
Jupiter	778.8	142,600
Saturn	1,427	120,200
Uranus	2,870	49,000
Neptune	4,497	49,500
Pluto	5,900	3,000

EARTH FACTS

Circumference round the Equator: 40,073 kilometres.

Circumference round the Poles: 40,007 kilometres.

Distance to centre of Earth: about 6370 kilometres.

Surface area: about 510,065,600 square kilometres; sea covers 71% of the surface of the Earth.

Average distance from the Sun: 149,600,000 kilometres; the Earth is farther away from the Sun in July than in January.

Rotation Speed: at the Equator, the Earth rotates on its axis at 1660 kilometres per hour.

Speed in orbit: The Earth travels at 29.8 kilometres per second.

Average distance from Moon: 385,000 kilometres.

DEEP, LONG AND HIGH

Greatest ocean depth:
Marianas trench, Pacific Ocean .. 11.033 m

Deepest underwater gorge:
near Esperance in Western
Australia .... 1800 m

Longest gorge:
Grand Canyon, Arizona, USA ..... 349 km

Highest navigated lake:
Titicaca, Peru/Bolivia .... 3810 m above
sea level

Deepest lake:
Baykal, Siberia, USSR .... 1620 m

AGES OF THE EARTH

Era, Period, Epoch	Years Ago
Pre-Cambrian time (life begins)	4600–570 million
Palaeozoic era (fish, amphibians and reptiles appear)	370–245 million
Cambrian Period	570–500 million
Ordovician Period	500–440 million
Silurian Period	440–395 million
Devonian Period	395–345 million
Carboniferous Period	345–280 million
Permian Period	280–245 million
Mesozoic era (age of dinosaurs)	245–65 million
Triassic Period	245–200 million
Jurassic Period	200–145 million
Cretaceous Period	145–65 million
Cenozoic era (age of mammals)	65–0 million
Tertiary Period	65–2 million
Palaeocene Epoch	65–60 million
Eocene Epoch	60–35 million
Oligocene Epoch	35–25 million
Miocene Epoch	25–5 million
Pliocene Epoch	5–2 million
Quaternary Period	2–0 million
Pleistocene Epoch	2 million–10,000
Holocene Epoch	10,000–0

LONGEST RIVERS

	km
Nile (Africa)	6690
Amazon (South America)	6570
Mississippi-Missouri (USA)	6212
Irtysh (USSR)	5570
Chang Jiang (Yangtze) (China)	5520
Hwang Ho (Yellow) (China)	4672
Zaire (Congo) (Africa)	4667
Amur (Asia)	4509
Lena (USSR)	4269
Mackenzie (Canada)	4241
Mekong (Asia)	4184
Niger (Africa)	4168

DESERTS

	sq km
Sahara	9,096,000
Australian Desert	1,550,000
Arabian Desert	1,300,000
Gobi Desert	1,295,000
Kalahari	520,000

LARGEST LAKES

	sq km
Caspian Sea (USSR/Iran)	370,898
Superior (USA/Canada)	82,814
Victoria Nyanza (Africa)	69,485
Aral (USSR)	68,682
Huron (USA/Canada)	59,596
Michigan (USA)	58,016
Tanganyika (Africa)	32,893
Baykal (USSR)	31,492
Great Bear (Canada)	31,328

LARGEST ISLANDS

	sq km
Greenland (Kalaallit Nunaat) (N. Atlantic)	2,175,600
New Guinea (S.W. Pacific)	821,090
Borneo (Kalimantan) (S.W. Pacific)	751,900
Madagascar (Indian Ocean)	587,041
Baffin I. (Canadian Arctic)	507,541
Sumatra (Indian Ocean)	473,607
Honshu (N.W. Pacific)	230,988
Great Britain (N. Atlantic)	229,522

OCEANS

	sq km
Pacific	181,000,000
Atlantic	106,000,000
Indian	73,481,000
Arctic	14,056,000

FAMOUS EARTHQUAKES

Shensi Province, China, 1556: Over 800,000 people perished – more than in any other earthquake.

Lisbon, Portugal, 1755: About 60,000 people died and shocks were felt as far away as Norway.

San Francisco, USA 1906: An earthquake and the fires it caused destroyed the city.

Kwanto Plain, Japan, 1923: Some 570,000 buildings collapsed. This was the costliest earthquake ever as measured by damage to property.

Lebu, Chile, 1977: The strongest earthquake shock ever recorded.

GEOGRAPHY TERMS

atmosphere The layer of moving air which surrounds the Earth. It consists of nitrogen, oxygen, water vapour and other gases.

canyon A deep, steep-sided valley, usually cut by a river in a *desert* area where the sides do not get very worn away by rain-water and streams.

climate The average weather conditions of a place.

coral Coral is made by tiny creatures called polyps which live in warm sunny seas. They build skeletons outside their bodies. When they die new polyps build on the old skeletons to form coral reefs.

delta The Greek letter Δ (delta), used to describe an area of sediments deposited at the mouth of some rivers.

deserts A dry area where little grows. Sometimes defined as an area with less than 250 mm (10 inches) of rain a year.

estuary The mouth of a river where it enters the sea.

fiord (fjord) A long, steep-sided inlet of the sea in a mountainous coastal area.

geyser (geysir) A hot spring which throws out a jet of hot water regularly or occasionally. Geysers occur in volcanic areas.

glacier A mass of ice which moves slowly downhill.

hurricane A severe tropical storm with spiralling winds of up to 340 km per hour and very low air pressure.

oasis An area in a desert with water at or near the surface.

peninsula An area of land almost surrounded by water.

plateau An upland area with a fairly level surface. Much of Eastern and Southern Africa is a plateau.

precipitation When used of weather, refers to rain or snow.

rain forest Tropical forest in hot rainy or monsoon areas.

savanna Tropical grassland where it is hot all through the year.

tropics Lines of latitude marking where the Sun is directly overhead on mid-summer's day. On 21 June, the Sun is overhead at the Tropics of Cancer. On 21 December, it is overhead at the Tropic of Capricorn.

tundra A treeless zone around the Arctic Circle.

wadi A dry watercourse in a desert.

AIRLINE LIVERIES

Aer Lingus
(Republic of
Ireland)

Aeroflot
(Soviet Union)

Air Canada
(Canada)

Air France
(France)

Air-India
(India)

Air Malta
(Malta)

Air New Zealand
(New Zealand)

Alitalia
(Italy)

Austrian Airlines
(Austria)

British Airways
(United Kingdom)

Cathay Pacific
(Hong Kong)

CSA
(Czechoslovakia)

El Al
(Israel)

Gulf Air
(Oman)

Iberia
(Spain)

Interflug
(East Germany)

raqi Airways
(Iraq)

Japan Air Lines
(Japan)

KLM
(Netherlands)

Korean Air
(S. Korea)

LOT
(Poland)

Lufthansa
(West Germany)

Olympic Airways
(Greece)

Pan Am
(United States)

Qantas
(Australia)

Sabena
(Belgium)

SAS
(Denmark, Norway,
Sweden)

Saudia
(Saudi Arabia)

apore Airlines
apore)

Swissair
(Switzerland)

TWA
(United States)

Varig
(Brazil)

MOTOR CAR INTERNATIONAL IDENTIFICATION LETTERS

A	Austria	GBM	Isle of Man*	RH	Haiti
ADN	Yemen PDR	GBZ	Gibraltar	RI	Indonesia*
AFG	Afghanistan	GCA	Guatemala	RIM	Mauritania
AL	Albania	GH	Ghana	RL	Lebanon
AND	Andorra	GR	Greece	RM	Madagascar
AUS	Australia*	GUY	Guyana*		(Malagasy Rep.)
B	Belgium	H	Hungary	RMM	Mali
BD	Bangladesh*	HK	Hong Kong*	RN	Niger
BDS	Barbados*	HKJ	Jordan	RO	Romania
BG	Bulgaria	I	Italy	ROK	South Korea
BH	Belize	IL	Israel	ROU	Uruguay
BR	Brazil	IND	India*	RP	Philippines
BRN	Bahrain	IR	Iran	RSM	San Marino
BRU	Brunei*	IRL	Ireland, Republic of*	RU	Burundi
BS	Bahamas*	IRQ	Iraq	RWA	Rwanda
BUR	Burma	IS	Iceland	S	Sweden
C	Cuba	J	Japan	SD	Swaziland*
CDN	Canada	JA	Jamaica*	SF	Finland
CH	Switzerland	K	Kampuchea	SGP	Singapore*
CI	Côte d'Ivoire	KWT	Kuwait	SME	Suriname*
CL	Sri Lanka*	L	Luxembourg	SN	Senegal
CO	Colombia	LAO	Laos	SU	USSR
CR	Costa Rica	LAR	Libya	SWA	
CS	Czechoslovakia	LB	Liberia	or ZA	} Namibia*
CY	Cyprus*	LS	Lesotho*	SY	Seychelles
D	West Germany	M	Malta*	SYR	Syria
DDR	East Germany	MA	Morocco	T	Thailand*
DK	Denmark	MAL	Malaysia*	TG	Togo
DOM	Dominican Rep.	MC	Monaco	TN	Tunisia
DY	Benin	MEX	Mexico	TR	Turkey
DZ	Algeria	MS	Mauritius*	TT	Trinidad and
E	Spain	MW	Malawi*		Tobago*
EAK	Kenya*	N	Norway	USA	United States
EAT	Tanzania*	NIC	Nicaragua	V	Vatican City
or EAZ		NL	Netherlands	VN	Vietnam
EAU	Uganda*	NZ	New Zealand*	WAG	Gambia
EC	Ecuador	P	Portugal	WAL	Sierra Leone
ES	El Salvador	PA	Panama	WAN	Nigeria
ET	Egypt	PAK	Pakistan*	WD	Dominica*
ETH	Ethiopia	PE	Peru	WG	Grenada*
F	France	PL	Poland	WL	St Lucia
FJI	Fiji*	PNG	Papua New Guinea	WS	Western Samoa
FL	Liechtenstein	PY	Paraguay	WV	St Vincent*
FR	Faroe Islands	RA	Argentina	YU	Yugoslavia
GB	Great Britain &	RB	Botswana*	YV	Venezuela
	Northern Ireland*	RC	Taiwan	Z	Zambia*
GBA	Alderney	RCA	Central African Rep.	ZA	South Africa*
GBG	Guernsey } Channel*	RCB	Congo	ZRE	Zaire
GBJ	Jersey } Islands	RCH	Chile	ZW	Zimbabwe*

*Drive on the left, otherwise drive on the right.

CAR BADGES

Chevrolet

Fiat

Rover

Lancia

Peugeot

Renault

Vauxhall

Cadillac

Audi

Ford

Mercedes-Benz

Volvo

Aston Martin

Rolls-Royce

Saab

M.G.

Porsche

Volkswagon

DATAFILE ON THE ARTS

BOOKS FOR PLEASURE

Anne of Green Gables, Lucy M. Montgomery
Ballet Shoes, Noel Streatfeild
Borrowers, The, Mary Norton
Children of Green Knowe, The, Lucy M. Boston
Children of the New Forest, The, Captain Marryat
Christmas Carol, A, Charles Dickens
Daisy Chain, The, Charlotte M. Yonge
David Copperfield, Charles Dickens
Eagle of the Ninth, The, Rosemary Sutcliffe
Family from One End Street, The, Eve Garnett
Good Wives, Louisa M. Alcott
Heidi, Johanna Spyri
Hereward the Wake, Charles Kingsley
Little Grey Rabbit, Alison Uttley
Little Lord Fauntleroy, Frances Hodgson Burnett
Little Tim and the Brave Sea Captain, Edward Ardizzone
Little Women, Louisa M. Alcott
Lorna Doone, R. D. Blackmore
Men of the Hills, Henry Treece
Marianne Dreams, Catherine Storr
Martin Pippin in the Daisy Field, Eleanor Farjeon
Minnow on the Say, Ann Philippa Pearce
Paddington Bear books, Michael Bond
Peacock House, The, Gillian Avery
Railway Children, The, E. Nesbit
Sampson's Circus, Howard Spring
Secret Garden, The, Frances Hodgson Burnett
Stig of the Dump, Clive King
Story of Holly and Ivy, Rumer Godden
Sunrise Tomorrow, Naomi Mitchison
Teddy Robinson books, Joan G. Robinson
We Didn't Mean to Go to Sea, Arthur Ransome
What Katy Did books, Susan Coolidge
Word to Caesar, Geoffrey Trease

ANIMAL STORIES

At the Back of the North Wind, George MacDonald
Babar The Little Elephant, Jean de Brunhoff
Bambi, Felix Salten
Black Beauty, Anna Sewell
Born Free, Joy Adamson
Call of the Wild, Jack London
Dog Toby, Richard Church

Jungle Book, The, Rudyard Kipling
Mousewife, The, Rumer Godden
One Hundred and One Dalmatians, Dodie Smith
Rufty Tufty books, Ruth Ainsworth
Snow Goose, The, Paul Gallico
Tarka the Otter, Henry Williamson
Watership Down, Richard Adams
White Fang, Jack London
Wind in the Willows, The, Kenneth Grahame

FANTASY STORIES

Alice's Adventures in Wonderland, Lewis Carroll
Andersen's Fairy Tales, Hans Christian Andersen
Book of Discoveries, A, John Masefield
English Fairy Tales, Joseph Jacobs
Five Children and It, E. Nesbit
Granny's Wonderful Chair, Frances Browne
Grimm's Fairy Tales, Brothers Grimm
Happy Prince and Others Stories, The, Oscar Wilde
Hobbit, The, J. R. R. Tolkien
Invisible Man, The, H. G. Wells
Lion, the Witch and the Wardrobe, The, C. S. Lewis
Little Grey Men, The, 'B. B.'
Magic Finger, The, Roald Dahl
Magic Walking Stick, The, John Buchan
Mary Poppins books, Pamela L. Travers
Oz books, L. Frank Baum
Peter Pan and Wendy, Sir James Barrie
Pinocchio, C. Collodi
Princess and the Goblin, The, George MacDonald
Puck of Pook's Hill, Rudyard Kipling
Rose and the Ring, The, William Makepeace Thackeray
Three Royal Monkeys, The, Walter de la Mare
Time Garden, The, Edward Eager
Tom's Midnight Garden, Ann Philippa Pearce
Twelve and the Genii, The, Pauline Clarke
Weirdstone of Brisingamen The, Alan Garner
Whispering Mountain, Joan Aiken
Witch Family, The, Eleanor Ruth Estes
Wizard of Earthsea, A, Ursula Le Guin

ADVENTURE STORIES

Adventures of Huckleberry Finn, The, Mark Twain

Coral Island, The, R. M. Ballantyne
Gulliver's Travels, Jonathan Swift
Hornblower books, C. S. Forester
Kept in the Dark, Nina Bawden
King Solomon's Mines, Rider Haggard
Moby Dick, Herman Melville
Moonfleet, J. Meade Falkner
Pilgrims of the Wild, 'Grey Owl'
Prisoner of Zenda, The, Anthony Hope
Robinson Crusoe, Daniel Defoe
Scarlet Pimpernel, The, Baroness Orczy
Smith, Leon Garfield
Swiss Family Robinson, W. H. G.
Kingston
Thirty-nine Steps, The, John Buchan
Treasure Island, Robert Louis Stevenson
Twenty Thousand Leagues Under the Sea,
Jules Verne
Uncle Tom's Cabin, Harriet Beecher
Stowe

HUMOROUS STORIES

Bad Child's Book of Beasts, The, Hilaire
Belloc
Book of Nonsense, A, Edward Lear
Charlie and the Chocolate Factory, Roald
Dahl
Father Christmas, Raymond Briggs
Helen's Babies, John Habberton
Just William, Richmal Crompton
Magic Pudding, The, Norman Lindsay
My Friend Mr Leakey, J. B. S. Haldane
Nonsense Novels, Stephen Leacock
North Winds Blow Free, Elizabeth
Howard
Now We are Six, A. A. Milne
Old Possum's Book of Practical Cats, T. S.
Eliot
Three Men in a Boat, Jerome K. Jerome
Wind on the Moon, The, Eric Linklater
Winnie-the-Pooh, A. A. Milne
Wombles books, Elisabeth Beresford

'POP' MUSIC

The term 'pop' is generally not used
today to describe all 'popular' (non-
classical) music. Jazz and folk are popular
forms that are usually considered
separately. Today's mass-market,
mainstream pop really started as 'rock
and roll' in the 1950s, which in turn grew
out of the fusion of black 'rhythm and
blues' and white 'country-and-western'
music.

SOME 'GREATS' OF POP

David Bowie (born 1947) British singer-
songwriter with powerfully imaginative
style and presentation.
Bob Dylan (born 1941) American singer-
songwriter who fused early 1960s folk
style with rock.
Jimi Hendrix (1942–70) American, often
said to be rock's all-time greatest
guitarist.
Buddy Holly (1936–59) American singer-
songwriter with simple, direct style. Very
short career.
Bob Marley (1945–81) Jamaican who, with
his group 'The Wailers', popularised
reggae music.
Elvis Presley (1935–77) American singer
who burst onto the scene in the 1950s
with 'new' music – rock 'n' roll. Rock's
first superstar.
Stevie Wonder (born 1950) American
singer-songwriter and musician, born
blind; major figure for 20 years.

TOP RECORDS

Greatest selling record to date is Irving
Berlin's *White Christmas*. Bing Crosby's
famous 1942 recording has sold 30 million
and more than 100 million copies of other
versions have been sold.
The greatest-selling 'pop' record to date
is *Rock Around the Clock*. Recorded in
1954 by Bill Haley and the Comets, it has
sold around 25 million copies.
The most successful group in terms of
record sales was the Beatles, from
Liverpool, England. The Beatles split up
in 1970. By summer 1985 estimates
showed that more than one billion
Beatles records and tapes had been sold.
   The next most successful group is
thought to be ABBA. These four Swedes
had sold 215 million records and tapes by
1985.

ARCHITECTS

Aalto Alvar	(1898–1976)
Finnish	
Adam, Robert	(1728–92)
Scottish	
Alberti, Leone Battista	(1404–72)
Italian	
Bernini, Gianlorenzo	(1598–1680)
Italian	
Bramante, Donato	(1444–1514)
Italian	
Brunelleschi, Filippo	(1377–1446)
Italian	
Cortona, Pietro da	(1596–1669)
Italian	
Fischer von Erlach, Johann	(1656–1723)
Austrian	
Gaudi, Antonio	(1852–1926)
Spanish	
Gropius, Walter	(1883–1969)
German	
Jefferson, Thomas	(1743–1826)
American	
Jones, Inigo	(1573–1652)
English	
Le Corbusier	(1887–1965)
French-Swiss	
Mansart, Francois	(1598–1666)
French	
Michelangelo, Buonarroti	(1475–1564)
Italian	
Mies van der Rohe, Ludwig	(1886–1969)
German/American	
Nash, John	(1752–1835)
English	
Nervi, Pier Luigi	(1891–1979)
Italian	
Niemayer, Oscar	(1907–)
Brazilian	
Palladio, Andrea	(1508–80)
Italian	
Saarinen, Eero	(1910–1961)
Finnish-American	
Wren, Sir Christopher	(1632–1723)
English	
Wright, Frank Lloyd	(1869–1959)
American	

Dome of
Florence
Cathedral
showing the
main ribs.

PERIODS OF ARCHITECTURE

Greek	60s–100s BC
Roman	100s BC–AD 400s
Byzantine	AD 400s–1453
Romanesque	
(N Europe)	mid-900s–late 1100s
Norman (England)	late 1000s–1100s
Gothic	mid-1100s–1400s
Renaissance (Italy)	1400s–1500s
French Renaissance	1500s
Baroque (Italy)	1600–1750
Georgian (England)	1725–1800
Rococo	mid-1700s
Regency (England)	1800–1825
Art Nouveau	
(Europe)	1890–1910
Expressionism	
(Germany)	1910–1930s
Functionalism	1920s–
International Style	1920s–
Brutalism	1950s–
Modern	1960s–
Post Modern	

FILM FEATS

Walt Disney (1901–66) holds the record number of Oscar awards – 32 including certificates, plaques etc.

Katharine Hepburn is the only person to win four Oscar awards in major roles.

All-time record for the highest value box office receipts – $312 million – is still held by the 1939 film *Gone With the Wind*, starring Vivien Leigh and Clark Gable.

THEATRE RECORDS

The longest continuous run of any play at one theatre ended on 23 March 1974, after 8860 performances of *The Mousetrap*, by Agatha Christie. Having spent 22 years at the Ambassador's Theatre, London, it moved to the St Martin's next door.

The oldest indoor theatre still in use is the Teatro Olimpico in Vicenza, Italy. Completed in 1583, it was designed according to the principles of the Roman writer Vitruvius by Andrea di Pietro (also called Palladio).

The first theatre in Britain was built by James Burbage in 1576, and called simply The Theatre. Later, it was dismantled and its timbers used to build Shakespeare's Globe Theatre.

The oldest national theatre in the world is the Comédie Française, established in 1680 by order of Louis XIV. It was formed by combining the three most important companies then playing in Paris.

MISCELLANEOUS DATAFILE

ANIMALS: LONGEVITY AND SPECIALIZED NAMES

	Life span (years)	Male	Female	Young	Group
Antelope	10	buck	doe	fawn	herd
Bear	15–50	boar	sow	cub	sleuth
Cat	15	tom	queen	kitten	cluster
Cattle	20	bull	cow	calf	herd
Deer	10–20	buck, hart, stag	doe, hind	fawn	herd
Dog	12–15	dog	bitch	puppy	kennel
Donkey	20	jack	jenny	foal	team
Duck	10	drake	duck	duckling	team
Elephant	60	bull	cow	calf	herd
Fox	10	dog-fox	vixen	cub	skulk
Giraffe	10–25	bull	cow	calf	herd
Goat	10	billy-goat	nanny-goat	kid	herd
Goose	25	gander	goose	gosling	skein (when in flight), gaggle
Hippopotamus	30–40	bull	cow	calf	herd
Horse	20–30	stallion	mare	foal	herd
Kangaroo	10–20	buck	doe	joey	mob
Lion	25	lion	lioness	cub	pride
Ostrich	50	cock	hen	chick	flock
Pig	10–15	boar	sow	piglet	drove
Rabbit	5–8	buck	doe	kit	warren
Rhinoceros	25–50	bull	cow	calf	crash
Sheep	10–15	ram	ewe	lamb	flock
Tiger	10–25	tiger	tigress	cub	
Whale	20	bull	cow	calf	school, pod
Zebra	20–25	stallion	mare	foal	herd

NAUTICAL MEASUREMENT

1 fathom = 6ft
1 nautical mile (international) = 1.151 statute mile (= 1852 metres)
60 nautical miles = 1 degree
1 knot = 1 nautical mile per hour

CONVERSION FACTORS

1 acre = 0.4047 hectares
1 centimetre = 0.3937 inch
1 cubic centimetre = 0.0610 cubic inch
1 cubic foot = 0.0283 cubic metre
1 cubic inch = 16.387 cubic centimetres
1 cubic metre = 35.3146 cubic feet
= 1.3079 cubic yards
1 cubic yard = 0.7646 cubic metre
1 fluid oz (apoth) = 28.4131 millilitres
1 foot = 0.3048 metre = 30.48 centimetres

DID YOU KNOW?

● There are around 600,000 words in the English language. An average person uses only a few thousand of these and a person can be fluent in English knowing only 2000 words. Professional writers know more words than average but even they only use 50,000 – less than 10% of the words available.

● Mandarin is the language spoken by most people – an estimated 600 million. English comes next and is spoken by about 360 million people world wide.

In just one second . . .

The world's population increases by three people.
The average person breathes in one seventh of a pint of air.
Concorde travels 600 metres.
The forcipomyia midge beats its wings 1,046 times.
A cheetah can run 30 metres.
A snail travels one millimetre.

CHEMICAL NAMES FOR SOME COMMON SUBSTANCES

Substance	Chemical name
Antifreeze	Ethylene glycol
Aspirin	Acetysalicylic acid
Baking powder	Sodium bicarbonate
Black lead	Graphite (a form of carbon)
Boracic acid	Boric acid
Borax	Sodium borate
Brimstone	Sulphur
Caustic soda	Sodium hydroxide
Chalk	Sodium carbonate
Common salt	Sodium chloride
Cream of tartar	Potassium bitartrate
DDT	Dichlor-diphenyl-trichlorethane
Epsom salts	Magnesium sulphate
Magnesia	Magnesium oxide
Plaster of Paris	Calcium sulphate
Potash	Potassium carbonate
Quick-lime	Calcium oxide
Quicksilver	Mercury
Saltpetre (nitre)	Potassium nitrate
Sal volatile	Ammonium carbonate
Talcum powder	Hydrated magnesium silicate
TNT	Trinitrotoluene
Vinegar	Dilute acetic acid
Washing soda	Crystalline sodium carbonate

ARABIC, ROMAN AND BINARY NUMERALS

Arabic	Roman	Binary	Arabic	Roman	Binary
1	I	1	40	XL	101000
2	II	10	50	L	110010
3	III	11	60	LX	111100
4	IV	100	64	LXIV	1000000
5	V	101	90	XC	1011010
6	VI	110	99	XCIX	1100011
7	VII	111	100	C	1100100
8	VIII	1000	200	CC	11001000
9	IX	1001	256	CCLVI	100000000
10	X	1010	300	CCC	100101100
11	XI	1011	400	CD	110010000
12	XII	1100	500	D	111110100
13	XIII	1101	512	DXII	1000000000
14	XIV	1110	600	DC	1001011000
15	XV	1111	900	CM	1110000100
16	XVI	10000	1000	M	1111101000
17	XVII	10001	1024	MXXIV	10000000000
18	XVIII	10010	1500	MD	10111011100
19	XIX	10011	2000	MM	11111010000
20	XX	10100	5000	$\overline{V}$	1001110001000
21	XXI	10101	10000	$\overline{X}$	10011100010000
29	XXIX	11101	20000	$\overline{X}\overline{X}$	100111000100000
30	XXX	11110	100000	$\overline{C}$	11000011010100000
32	XXXII	100000			

WEDDING ANNIVERSARIES

1st	Cotton	25th	Silver
5th	Wood	40th	Ruby
10th	Tin	50th	Gold
15th	Crystal	60th	Diamond
20th	China	70th	Platinum

SEVEN DEADLY SINS

The major sins listed by early Christians and medieval teachers, were Covetousness, Envy, Gluttony, Lust, Pride, Sloth, Wrath. They were frequently represented by characters in the morality plays.

SEVEN WONDERS OF THE ANCIENT WORLD

The Seven Wonders of the Ancient world were selected by the Greek poet Antipater of Sidon about the year 3 BC.

The Pyramids of Egypt
Built as tombs for Egyptian kings and queens in the 2000's BC the pyramids of Egypt are the only one of the original Seven Wonders that still remain.

The Hanging Gardens of Babylon
The hanging gardens were built on terraces at Babylon in Iraq about 600 BC by King Nebuchadnezzar to please his wife Amytis.

The Temple of Artemis (Diana) at Ephesus
Temple built at Ephesus, Turkey in 350 BC. It was destroyed by the Goths in 262 AD.

The Statue of Zeus (Jupiter) at Olympia
A 12-metre tall statue of the Greek god Zeus made of gold, marble and ivory by the sculptor Phidias in the 5th century BC.

The Tomb of Mausolus
A magnificent tomb completed in 325 BC in Halicarnassus (now Bodrum), Turkey for the body of King Mausolus of Caria by his widow Queen Artemisia.

The Colossus of Rhodes
This was a gigantic statue of the sun-god Helios (Apollo), 35 metres high, which spanned the entrance to the harbour at Rhodes. It was destroyed by an earthquake in 224 BC.

The Pharos of Alexandria
The Pharos of Alexandria was a lighthouse on an island in the harbour of Alexandria. It was built in 270 BC and destroyed by an earthquake in 1375 AD.

THE TWELVE LABOURS OF HERACLES (HERCULES)

In classical mythology Hercules was given 12 labours by Eurystheus with the promise that he would become immortal if he accomplished them. They were:

To kill the Nemean Lion.
To kill the Lernean hydra.
To capture the hind of Artemis.
To capture the Erymanthian boar.
To cleanse the Augean stables in a day.
To kill the man-eating Stymphalian birds.
To capture the Cretan bull.
To capture the man-eating mares of the Thracian Diomedes.
To seize the girdle of the Amazon queen Hippolyta.
To capture the oxen of Geryones in Erythia.
To steal the apples from the garden of the Hesperides.
To bring Cerberus up from the lower world.

THE TWELVE APOSTLES

These were the 12 followers – disciples – of Jesus Christ.

Peter (Simon)
Andrew
James the Less
John the Evangelist
Philip of Bethsaida
Bartholomew
Thomas (also known as Didymus)
Matthew (also known as Levi)
Simon the Canaanite (also known as Simon Zelotes)
Jude (also known as Judas and Thaddaeus)
James the Greater
Judas Iscariot

SEVEN HILLS OF ROME

The hills on which ancient Rome was built were: Palatine, Capitoline, Quirinal, Caelian, Aventine, Esquiline, Viminal.

COOKING

Ounces	Recommended conversion in grams	Ounces	Recommended conversion in grams
1	25	9	250
2	50	10	275
3	75	11	300
4	100	12	350
5	150	13	375
6	175	14	400
7	200	15	425
8	225	16 (1lb)	450

Oven temperatures: The table below gives recommended equivalents.

	°C	°F	Gas Mark
Very cool	110	225	$\frac{1}{4}$
	120	250	$\frac{1}{2}$
Cool	140	275	1
	150	300	2
Moderate	160	325	3
	180	350	4
Moderately hot	190	375	5
	200	400	6
Hot	220	425	7
	230	450	8
Very hot	240	475	9

ASTROLOGICAL SIGNS

CAPRICORN
December 22–January 19

AQUARIUS
January 20–February 18

PISCES
February 19–March 20

ARIES
March 21–April 19

TAURUS
April 20–May 20

GEMINI
May 21–June 20

CANCER
June 21–July 22

LEO
July 23–August 22

VIRGO
August 23–September 22

LIBRA
September 23–October 22

SCORPIUS
October 23–November 21

SAGITTARIUS
November 22–December 21

Greek			Russian	
Letter	Name	Transliteration	Letter	Transliteration
A α	alpha	a	А а	a
B β	beta	b	Б б	b
Γ γ	gamma	g	В в	v
Δ δ	delta	d	Г г	g
E ε	epsilon	e	Д д	d
Z ζ	zeta	z	Е е	e, ye
H η	eta	ē	Ж ж	zh
Θ θ	theta	th	З з	z
I ι	iota	i	И и	i
K κ	kappa	k	Й й	ı
Λ λ	lambda	l	К к	k
M μ	mu	m	Л л	l
N ν	nu	n	М м	m
Ξ ξ	xi	x (ks)	Н н	n
O o	omicron	o	О о	o
Π π	pi	p	П п	p
P ρ	rho	r	Р р	r
Σ σ.ς*	sigma	s	С с	s
T τ	tau	t	Т т	t
Υ υ	upsilon	u, y	У у	u
Φ φ	phi	ph	Ф ф	f
X χ	chi	kh. ch	Х х	kh
Ψ ψ	psi	ps	Ц ц	ts
Ω ω	omega	o	Ч ч	ch
			Ш ш	sh
			Щ щ	shch
			ы	i
			ь	'
			Э э	e
			Ю ю	yu
			Я я	ya

INDEX

Photographic Acknowledgements

The publishers would like to thank the following for kindly
supplying photographs for this book:

Page 16 ZEFA; 18 The Hutchison Library; 19 NHPA/ANT; 21
ZEFA (top) Remote Source/M. Jordan (bottom); 22 The
Hutchison Library (top) South American Pictures (bottom); 23
ZEFA; 57 ZEFA; 76 Nik Cookson; 84 Popperfoto; 89 Spectrum
Colour Library; 93 ZEFA; 97 Sonia Halliday Photographs; 122
ZEFA (top) Ancient Art & Architecture Collection (bottom);
134 Brian Furzer; 148 George Beal; 161 Colorsport (top)
Supersport (bottom); 167 Dev O'Neill/US Congress.